Samuel Wood

**The forcing garden**

or, How to grow early fruits, flowers and vegetables

Samuel Wood

**The forcing garden**
*or, How to grow early fruits, flowers and vegetables*

ISBN/EAN: 9783337375003

Printed in Europe, USA, Canada, Australia, Japan

Cover: Foto ©Lupo / pixelio.de

More available books at **www.hansebooks.com**

# THE FORCING GARDEN

OR

## HOW TO GROW EARLY FRUITS, FLOWERS, AND VEGETABLES:

WITH PLANS AND ESTIMATES SHOWING THE BEST AND MOST
ECONOMICAL WAY OF BUILDING GLASS-HOUSES, PITS,
AND FRAMES FOR THE VARIOUS CLASSES:

CONTAINING ALSO

ORIGINAL PLANS FOR DOUBLE GLAZING
ON THE VERTICAL BAR WITHOUT PUTTY; A NEW
METHOD OF GROWING THE GOOSEBERRY UNDER GLASS;
THE OPEN WALL-PEACH PROTECTOR, THE LILY-OF-THE-VALLEY
AND CHRISTMAS ROSE PIT COMBINED; WITH NUMEROUS
ORIGINAL CONTRIVANCES FOR VENTILATION,
AND FOR PROTECTING VINE BORDERS.

### With Illustrations.

## By SAMUEL WOOD,

AUTHOR OF 'GOOD GARDENING,' 'MULTUM-IN-PARVO GARDENING,'
'THE TREE PLANTER,' 'THE TREE PRUNER,' ETC.

### Second Edition.

Capio Lumen

## LONDON:
## CROSBY LOCKWOOD AND SON,
7 STATIONERS'-HALL COURT, LUDGATE HILL.
1898.

# PREFACE.

SEVERAL cogent reasons might be adduced for writing
the present work, the chief being a deep conviction
that something of the kind was really needed, to show
the best and most economical way of constructing
glass-houses, pits, &c., and the most desirable angle on
which to pitch the roofs of them, according to the
particular class of plants to be grown ; as well as the
best aspect in which to place such houses. It will be
observed that all my angles for fruit-growing are at a
very sharp pitch. This is, I think, most desirable for the
production not only of fine fruit but also for the kind
of wood that will ensure a good crop of fruit, especially
in the case of Peaches, Plums, and Grapes.

I am fully convinced of the necessity of a work like
this for nearly all classes who require sound information both for building glass-houses and for their subsequent adaptation. My method of double-glazing will,
I think, meet a want long felt, and no doubt will be
generally adopted for early forcing; my vine border-
protector will also doubtless supersede the usual method

of planting vines inside houses, being more accessible
for manuring the roots of them, and what is more important, the roots can get the full benefit of the sun
and air, and this is no doubt very necessary in all fruit-
growing, especially with stone fruit and Grapes ; for
Grape-growing, moisture combined with sun-heat is
most essential.

I have studied for a long time the functionary construction and the active properties of plants, especially
the vine, and I think I may say that I have found that
warmth combined with moisture at the roots are the
necessary conditions for well-coloured and fine fruit,
an abundance of oxygen among the branches being
likewise necessary for a good crop of fruit for the
coming year. On these principles I have established
my sharp angles and vine border-protector.

I believe it will be found that ' The Asparagus Pit,'
' The Lily of the Valley and Christmas Rose Pit,' ' The
Gooseberry House,' ' The Potato House,' 'The Pea
Frame,' and ' The Wall Peach Screens,' will recommend
themselves, and be regarded as something new, and of
some importance in their various capacities. The
method of getting large onions, and in greater numbers
will doubtless be a novelty with many persons.

My method of glazing with ' clips,' will be found
equal if not superior to most others; and the plans,
and careful estimates attached to the various arrange-
ments for building, glazing, and heating, will I hope
meet the wants of the horticultural enquirer.

# CONTENTS.

---

## PART I.

### *CULTIVATION OF THE VINE.*

---

## PART II.

### *ORCHARD HOUSES AND GLASS HOUSES.*

## PART III.

### THE EARLY FORCING OF VEGETABLES.

## CHAPTER V.

ON FORCING THE CARROT AND
FRENCH BEANS.

## CHAPTER VI.

ON FORCING THE MUSHROOM

## CHAPTER VII.

PAGE
HOW TO GET EARLY AND LARGE
ONIONS

## CHAPTER VIII.

ON WATERING PLANTS, ETC.

# PART IV.

*MONTHLY CALENDAR FOR THE FORCING GARDEN.*

THE

# FORCING GARDEN.

## INTRODUCTORY CHAPTER.

As a rule our natural fruits come at a time when they are not very much wanted. In hot countries they ripen in time to meet the real wants of the inhabitants ; but in a country like England most fruits, or at least the bulk of them, ripen late, when the heat of the summer is over. To meet this state of things much has been done of late years in the way of growing them under glass, and a great deal of this desirable manner of cultivating them is due to that popular and successful fruit-tree grower, the late Mr. Rivers, who has written so much on the subject.

There are, popularly speaking, three modes of growing fruits—viz. the original one, consisting of open-air culture ; the second is by means of the cold orchard house ; and the third by subjecting the trees to artificial heat, that is, applying heat by means of hot water, flues, or stoves ; and at the present time even gas stoves are recommended, but this last method will I fear prove not

B

only dangerous, but in some instances fatal. Why so? some will ask. The answer is, because if at any time a leakage as small even as a pin's head should occur either in the pipes or the stove, enough gas will escape to destroy every plant in the house. Gas stoves for plant houses are therefore very objectionable.

For economy, I know of no better system for amateurs and for plant work generally, than what is called the air-drain plan. The next best method is by means of hot-water pipes. The former is not adapted to fruit-forcing on a large scale, nor even for plant growing beyond forty feet in length; but for a house thirty feet long I believe it to be the most economical plan of all. However, for fruit forcing there is nothing so good as hot-water pipes; and to be really successful in forcing at all, whether with flowers or fruits, the grand point is to adapt the house to the subject, and not to make the subject subservient to the house: this is where so many persons fail.

It frequently happens that a man who has more money than experience in either fruit or plant growing (especially forcing), puts up a house or two for a certain purpose, say grape growing or the cultivation of the peach, which are no more adapted for such a purpose than a cow is likely to catch a hare. I always consider that the adaptation of the house to the object in view is almost, or I might say quite, an essential thing to ensure success. Common hot-house builders are generally the architects of these structures, men who know nothing whatever about even ordinary plant growing, much less about forcing of any kind: this is why we see such perverse kinds of glass structures with which a good gardener is often disgusted. I have seen whole sets of houses of this kind. A good gardener should be the architect of all glass and plant houses. Then the next thing is the aspect of them and the angle of the roof, and finally the best means of heating the particular kinds of houses so as to suit the respective subjects.

# PART I.

## *CULTIVATION OF THE VINE.*

## CHAPTER I.

### THE GRAPE HOUSE.

THE situation and pitch of the roof, especially the pitch, have a deal to do with success in the cultivation of the vine. If the ground is flat, a sharper pitch in the angle for the roof is necessary than is required for a steep incline in the surface, on account of the deadness of the surrounding vapour on a flat above that of an incline. A flat roof, or at least a roof with an angle of less than 45°, is not good for grape growing. Generally roofs are much less than that; but this angle and above that, are much the best for this purpose.

Some persons will object to this sharp pitch for forcing purposes, on account of the more rapid ascension of the heat to the higher part of the roof; but if sufficient heat is generated at the lower part so as to keep up a good temperature according to what is required for the circulation, one that will keep the house healthy and produce fine coloured fruit will be ensured.

It is the maintenance of a brisk circulation of heated air which colours grapes, and not the generally supposed high degree of heat without much circulation. If anyone wants proof of this, let him go to Texas, a country abounding with wild grapes, where they grow in vast quantities on the forest trees, the vines climbing about and over the tall pines. The temperature

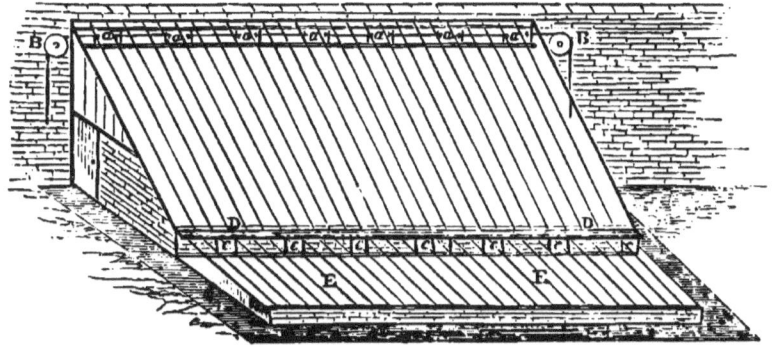

FIG. 1.—SECTION OF A SIXTY-FEET EARLY VINERY. FOURTEEN FEET HIGH AT THE BACK, TWO FEET HIGH IN FRONT, TWELVE FEET WIDE; TO BE DOUBLE-GLAZED WITHOUT PUTTY, WITH TWENTY-ONE-OUNCE GLASS, TWENTY BY EIGHTEEN.

Reference to plan.—a a a, sliding ventilators, worked by wires, and cords, and pulleys, B B. (See enlarged section of these ventilators, FIG. 2.) c c c c c c, two by one foot sliding shutters in front wall to work the same as the top ventilators. (See FIG. 3.) D D, flap shutter hinged on wall plate, to open by cords, for the admission of air to the house through the openings, 'c.' This flap shutter is on the vine-border protector, 'E' 'E.' This house is at an angle of 45°. THE BORDER PROTECTOR, E E, may be glazed with clips. which offer every facility for taking out the glass in May by merely loosening them, so as to lift the glass out, and leaving the clips there for reglazing in the autumn, which is quickly done. Taking the glass out in May admits of the border getting the benefit of the summer air and rains. The border protector may be made into sashes, which can be drawn off occasionally to allow of the rains falling on the borders, watering, &c.

there averages for months 90°, but the vines are surrounded with air, and although the heat is during the day often as much as 110°, the nights are very cool. These grapes are as black as jet. Here then is the secret of grape colouring—a heated circulation of pure air. This is what we want in our vineries, instead of

which they are heated to a good growing temperature
The grapes swell, but do not often colour well, especially the very early ones, and the reason is given
above.

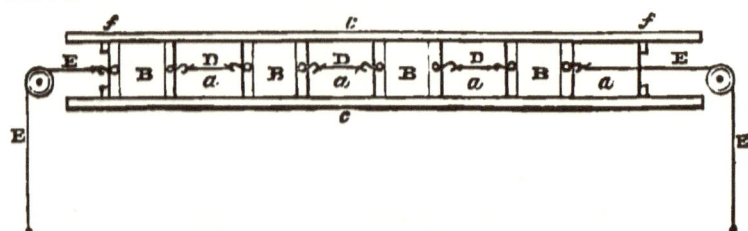

FIG. 2.—SECTION OF TOP VENTILATORS, TWO FEET SQUARE.

Reference to ventilators.—*a a a a*, openings in back wall of house close under wall
plate at the top ; B B B B, shutter and sliding ventilators ; *cc*, the runs in which
the ventilators slide, by means of connecting wires, D D D ; and the cords and
pulleys, E E E E ; *ff*, stops. The runs must be fixed on the wall with stout hooks,
and the pulleys fixed firmly on the wall. All these shutters can be opened and
shut at once the whole length of the house.

It is difficult ordinarily to get air enough into
very early graperies so as to colour the fruit. Houses
for the early forcing of vines are not constructed for the
safe admission of air in a sufficient quantity to colour

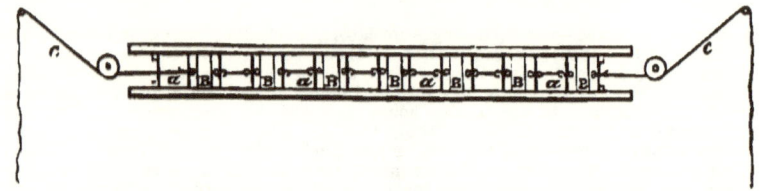

FIG. 3.—SECTION OF FRONT AIR SLIDING SHUTTERS FOR AN EARLY FORCING HOUSE
AND VINERY.

Reference.—*a a a a*, openings, one foot square, in front wall, as shown in sectional
plan of vinery (fig. 4), at ' B.' These openings may be four feet apart, or less.
B B B B B B B, sliding shutters, opened and shut all at once by the cords and
pulleys, *cc*. As these shutters are fixed so low, the cords work upwards instead of
pulling downwards, as in the case of the ventilators at the top of the house. They
may be outside.

the fruit well. The roofs are too flat for a brisk circulation, when it can be admitted, which is not often.
It will be seen in fig. 4 what my plan is for meeting

the case. This house is on a scale of one-sixteenth of an inch to a foot, and at an angle of 45°.

These bottom openings in the front wall can be safely left open almost constantly durirg the ripening of the grapes in cases of early forcing, for no chilly air can come to the tender growth of the vine. The air coming in direct contact with the hot pipes gets warmed, made lighter, and quickened. The heat of the pipes gives vitality to the air which is admitted; it ascends with rapidity to the fruit and branches,

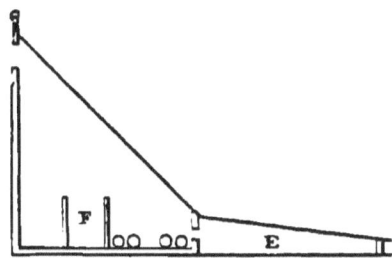

FIG. 4.—END SECTION.

Scale ₁⁄₁₆th inch to 1 foot.

and, there being a constant and fresh supply from the outside, it is well supplied with colouring matter, oxygen, which *must* be admitted or the grapes cannot possibly colour. The more of this you can safely admit combined with heat, the deeper will be the colour of the fruit, and the sweeter also. F, pit, 5 feet wide, the whole length of the house, to be filled with some fermenting material, such as leaves, stable manure, &c., to cause a damp and warm heat, which will materially facilitate the development of the vines and the fruit, in its first stage. E (fig. 4), root protection lights over the border, to be used through the winter and cold spring months : these are most essential in early forcing. I propose that the bars for this root protection for vine borders should. be fixed from the front wall 20 inches apart, and then glazed on my own plan without side laps or putty. (See illustration.)

As soon as the month of May comes, take the glass off and put it into boxes till it is wanted again, when the border will be open to all the genial influences of the sun, as well as the refreshing rains of the summer months. It is but a few hours' work for any good ordinary man to unglaze the whole of these border protectors, and to reglaze them, the 'clips' being already there.

For those who prefer them, shifting sashes may be used, which may be made to slide, as in the case of ordinary frame sashes, but these will cost double the expense of making. Air can be admitted by having a flap shutter one foot wide all along the eaves of the roof of the vinery, being made to open and shut by cords from the inside, above the pipes. If the border glass is arranged on my plan, this will be found to be the best, there being no lattice-like cross-bars, no side laps, nor so much glass as in all the other patent plans of glazing.

The ventilators in the wall, fig. 2, will, I have no doubt, be found the cheapest to construct, and the most convenient to work, as they can all be opened and shut at once, and that by a boy. A frame should be constructed so as to fix inside each opening in the wall and made to come beyond the brickwork a little, just enough to form a facing for the shutter, so that each one will fit sufficiently close to exclude the air and to prevent the escape of heat. The sliding shutter in the back cannot be made to shut close enough for early forcing on the bare brickwork or plaster unless the plaster of the wall is very fine, and the wall perfectly flat, so that they can fit as close as the lid of a box. This is quite necessary for early forcing.

The cost of this vinery is not so much as might be supposed. I can construct a house like this at less than thirty per cent. of the usual cost of single glazing with putty, taking everything into account. There is the saving in bricks by constructing hollow walls, fixed rafters, glazing without putty, and further economy by the adoption of my ventilators, and by the use of a cheap and improved heating apparatus.

Of course the house should not be built upon high and exposed ground where cold and cutting winds from the east or the west can play upon it unchecked. It should be situated on either low ground, or that of a medium level. If on a low level, good and thorough drainage must be secured both for the house and for the vines, so that no stagnant vapour shall be there to engender mildew. If, however, it must be built upon a level above the medium, choice should be made of a full southern aspect, and sheltered on the east and west sides by distant trees, but not nearer to the vinery than from 80 to 100 feet. In the western counties of England I find that the westerly winds do more harm to the foliage of various trees and shrubs during the summer and early autumn than the east winds; and even a vinery on a high and exposed place open to some of these fierce westerly winds would no doubt feel the bad effects more or less. But in the more easterly and northern counties, almost every early plant and plant-house and forcing house feels the spring

winds from the east, so that these two points require
to be guarded against in the case of early vineries.

### THE BACK WALLS.

Should there be no wall suitable for the construction of an early vinery, one must be built for a lean-to
house; for one of these at a good sharp pitch is far

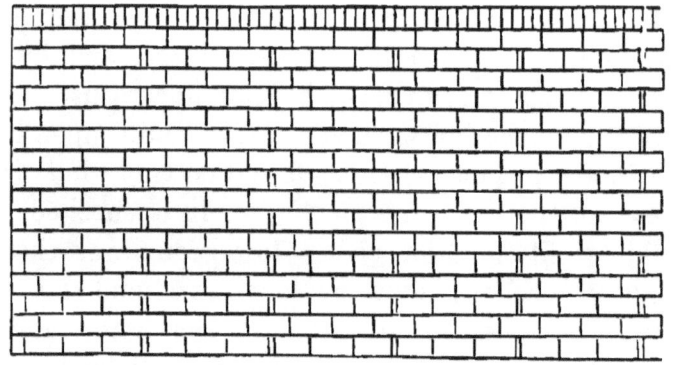

FIG. 5.—TWELVE BY SIX FEET SECTION OF CAVITY WALL, NINE INCHES THICK.
THE BRICKS ARE BUILT UP ON THE SIDES, AND NOT LAID FLAT, AS IS USUAL
WITH COMMON BRICKWORK.

|  | £ | s. | d. |
|---|---|---|---|
| A wall on this plan of building, sixty feet long, twelve feet high, and nine inches thick, will cost for the bricks, at 1l. 10s., carriage included | 8 | 0 | 0 |
| Labour (one week for mason) . . . . . | 1 | 10 | 0 |
| Man (one week) . . . . . . . | 0 | 15 | 0 |
| Lime and sand . . . . . . . . | 0 | 7 | 0 |
|  | £10 | 12 | 0 |

superior for an early house than a span or half span.    I
feel convinced of this, for be it remembered that when
the house contains a good, dry back wall, and the roof
of it is lying well towards the early spring sun, the
wall absorbs so much of the rays that it will materially

augment the heat of the interior of the house, and, being of uncoloured brick, it will continue to give out

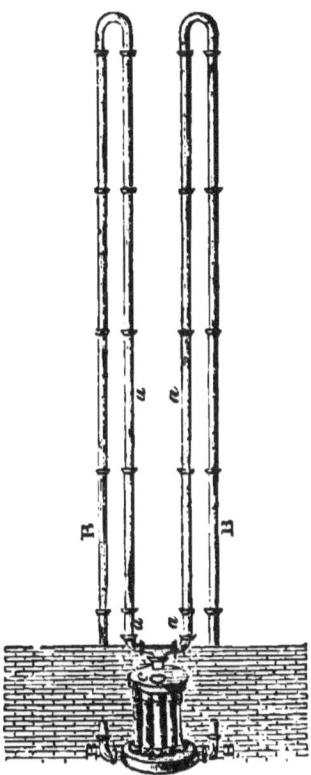

FIG. 6.—BOILER AND SECTION OF PIPES FOR EARLY VINERY.

Reference.—*a a*, flow pipes ; B B B B, return pipes. All the pipes should be six-inch. The cost of this apparatus may be estimated at—

|  | £ | s. | d. |
|---|---|---|---|
| For the boiler | 6 | 0 | 0 |
| Two hundred and forty feet of six-inch pipe, at 2*s*. 3*d*. per foot | 26 | 18 | 0 |
| Two syphon bends | 1 | 5 | 0 |
| Four elbows | 1 | 15 | 0 |
| As many indiarubber rings wanted as there are joints ; a cistern, and bricks, and the setting, which may be computed at about | 6 | 0 | 0 |
|  | £41 | 18 | 0 |

heat for hours after sunset. When however there is no such wall a great deal is lost in this respect.

No early vinery should contain too much glass. When I say ' too much,' I mean that there should be none on the cold sides. There is nothing like a good dry brick wall for the back of an early vinery, with but little or no glass at the ends. A house constructed on my plan, *i.e.* at the angle above named, will be abundantly light enough without any more glass than what the roof contains, and will be better adapted for maintaining the necessary heat at a less cost.

In constructing a back wall, it will be a great advantage in every way to build it according to my method, that is, hollow. A wall constructed on this plan, 60 feet long, 12 feet high, and 9 inches thick, will take about 5,360 bricks; while one of the same dimensions built with solid work, as is usually done, will take 7,930 or thereabouts. Here then is a difference of 2,570 bricks in the first place, and then there is a saving of at least 1*l.* in mason's and mason's labourer s wages and mortar. Nor is this all, for a wall so constructed is much drier, and therefore of necessity much warmer; the wall is full of chambers of heated air, which continue to give out their contents by night into the house, which is an immense advantage in early work, as by this means a better result is obtained than by a fire-heated flue. In virtue of such a wall, the angle of roof, and the construction of an apparatus like that shown in fig. 6, I may challenge all others, that is, supposing the roof to be double-glazed on my plan, and having the ' border protector.'

*THE CHEAPEST AND BEST METHOD OF GLAZING GRAPE
HOUSES ETC. WITHOUT PUTTY.*

Figs. 7, 8, 9.   There is no doubt that this plan
of glazing all houses is the best both for cheapness

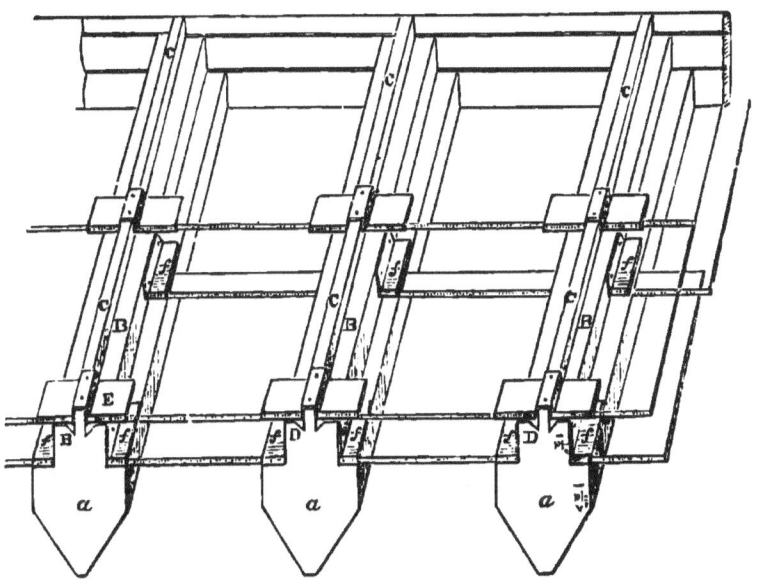

FIG. 7.—SECTIONAL VIEW OF MY PATENT COMPRESS CLIP AND SCREW
DOUBLE GLAZING.

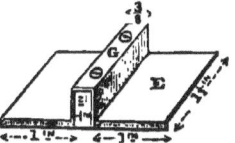

Reference.— *a a a*, rafter ; B B B, bed for top squares : C C C, half-inch 'standard
rebate,' and three-eighths of an inch wide. for a butt for glass, to make the top
glazing wind- and water-tight ; D D D, grooves to take off any wet that may get in
at the top ; E E, the metal clip and screws ; *f f f*, the metal clip for under layer of
glass, fastened on the rebate with two small tacks.  The screws need not be more
than five-eighths of an inch long, clear from the head, which should be rounded
at the top, and broad and flat underneath.  They may be of *galvanised iron* or
*brass* ; and when at any time a square has to be replaced, a small screw-driver
will draw the screw, ' G,' a little, so as to release the glass, when it can be removed
without lifting the clip off, and the new square of glass slipped in, the clip being
gently screwed down again : all of which can be done within five minutes.  This
method is perfectly immovable as regards wind, and quite air-tight-

of construction and economy, as well as for effect. The top layer of glass may be employed for single work,

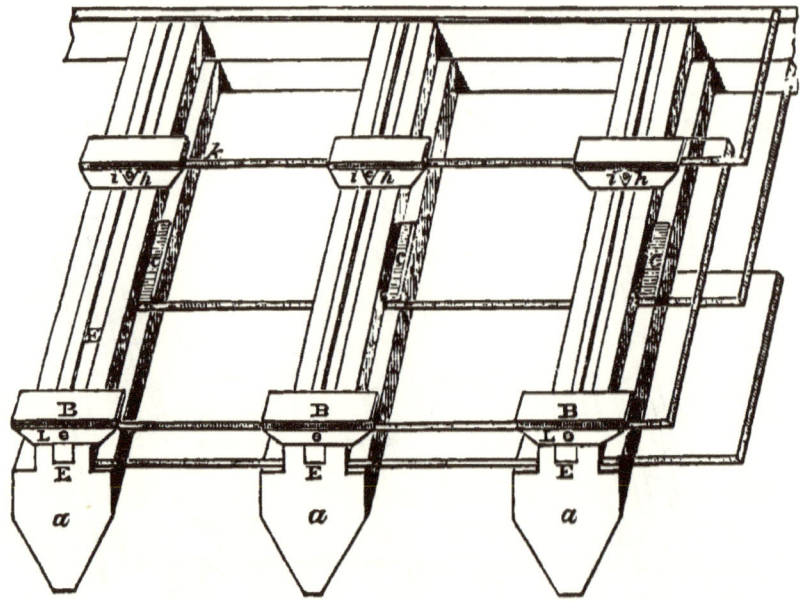

Fig. 8.—Sectional view of metal clip and screw glazing without putty without outside rebate.

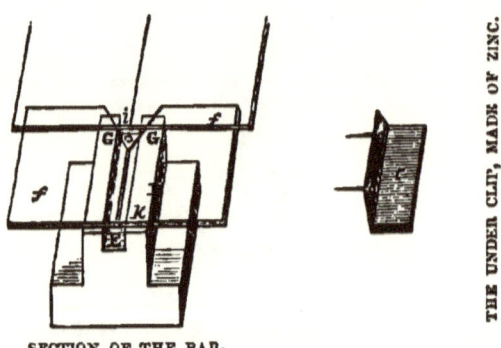

SECTION OF THE BAR.

THE UNDER CLIP, MADE OF ZINC.

Reference.—*a a a*, the rafter; B B B, the top clips and screw; *c c c*, the clips for under squares, nailed on the rebate, 'D;' E E, the groove in top of rafter to take any water; *f f*, the glass with the corner cut off, exactly as is shown at G G; and marked on the clip at '*h*,' to admit of the screw, *i*. These cut corners come underneath the lap, *k*, except a piece to admit of the screw, and that is covered by the lower end of the clip, L.

and the under layer added for double glazing. All the difference in expense lies merely in the cost of the glass, which is a trifle compared with the use of two layers instead of one in early forcing.

All good gardeners will doubtless see the advantages attached to the plan of double glazing, and I have

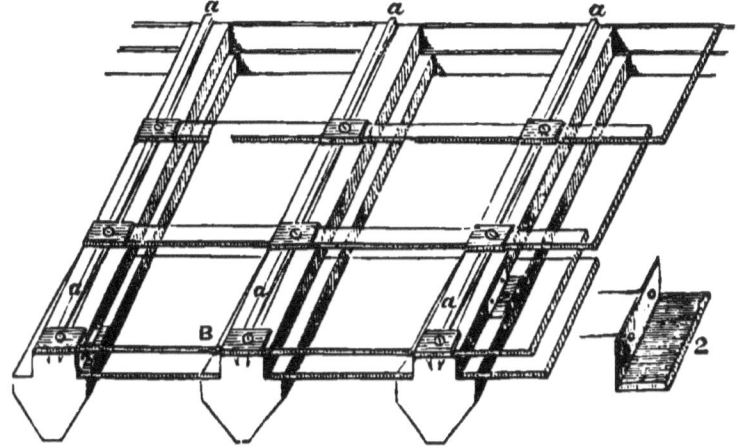

FIG. 9.—SECTIONAL VIEW OF DOUBLE GLAZING, WITH SPRING BRASS CLI
AND SCREW.

As in fig. No. 7, but with rebate, letter a, rising one and a half eighth of an inch, or the thickness of double glass, so that the edges can butt up to it, thus rendering the glazing perfectly air-tight. The standards, a a a, need not be more than one-quarter of an inch wide, the screws, B, going through it. The under layer of glass is held in position by the thin metal clips, as in the illustration 2.

no doubt that, if this is done without putty, or any other material that will prevent the water from condensing into vapour, it will be seen at a glance that this method while perfectly air-tight is not retentive of water in the roof of the house, which when frosts occur materially lowers the temperature of the place. This is especially the case in single glazing, where extra fires must be kept up to keep out the frost. It is not necessary for me to say here that frost has a material and additional influence upon everything exposed to it, when wet or damp more than when it is dry.  The practical man will know at once how to appreciate the double glazing above the single, on account of the under glazing being preserved dry, which no single method can do.

Single glazing may be employed for all cool orchard houses, vineries, cool plant houses, &c. ; but I recommend all forcing houses  and tender exotic plant houses to be double-glazed on one of the plans illustrated and described in this work.

# CHAPTER II.

IT is very necessary to make a good preparation before planting vines in the first instance; but the way it is to be done is a matter on which great diversity of opinion exists. I have known many vines ruined by packing strong stimulants upon their roots. It is quite a mistake to plant young vines, in the first instance, in undecomposed animal matter. It is another mistake, too, merely to make a vine border of only about six or eight feet in width and then to confine the roots to that limited space, composed, it may be, of very fatty matter, burying it five or six feet deep. Let any man examine the roots of vines so treated and he will find that they are mere fibreless channels except at the extremities, which possess a few spongioles of a healthy nature simply because they have saved themselves from the surcharge of the acid compounds and were buried so deep that some purifying influences could reach them and render them sufficiently nutritious for the real benefit of the vines. On examination of the roots of vines of five or more years so situated, it will be seen that the young fibrous roots—the life of the whole plant, and on which are found the spongioles or feeders—have made their way to those parts of the bed where less of the superabounding fatty matter is to

C

be found, such parts being of a more intermediate condition, and where the sun and air exert their influence.

It will be found on examination that the roots of a
vine planted inside a house where the bed of the house
is made of the best material from the front to the
back, if the vines are planted at the front the roots will
crowd and cling to the front wall, and creep along the
wall in search of a way out—and out they will get if
possible. And why? Because they love the sun and
free air. Now go outside and carefully search the surface of the ground an inch or two deep, and if the vines
have been planted, say, five, seven, or ten years, you
will find the fibrous roots twenty or thirty feet from
the main stem, a little under the surface; and if there
should by any means be a common sewer, foul ditch,
pool, or anything of that sort near, it will be found that
the spongioles have dipped their mouths only, into the
contents just at the edges, unless they are half dry, or
nearly so, then they may be further advanced; but, as
a rule, it will be observed that no really sound roots of
a hard and durable kind can exist in a deep mass of
rich fatty matter where no sun, heat, or oxidising air
can get to them.

Moisture is absolutely necessary for the well-being
of the vine; but to surcharge the tender fibre with it
will ultimately be its death. Besides, the mischief
will show itself in various forms—such as mildew,
shanking of the berries, and, finally, general weakness.
I have lately had to do with some fine vines, twenty or
more years old, which are planted on a hill facing the
south. The soil is naturally poor, with a narrow vine-
border of about six feet or so wide. They are planted
outside, and next to the border comes a broad carriage

road, and beyond that nothing but a poor, half-kept grass lawn fifty or sixty feet wide; yet more healthy and vigorous vines, bearing as fine fruit as can be wished for, cannot be found. They are free from mildew or any kind of disease, notwithstanding a most unfavourable season. I attribute all this, not to a richly prepared border, but to the influence of the sun upon the roots lying under the gravel road immediately in front of the vinery, thus preserving a healthy and sound fibre ; and it is impossible to come to any other conclusion.

Now I think it will be evident that what is wanted before planting vines, is a good preparation on a broad scale. From my own experience I do not find a deep and superabundantly rich fatty matter confined to a limited space answer best ; but that the ground for an unlimited space should be made good by manuring it well with cow-dung (not horse-dung, for that will generate fungi of various kinds according to what the natural soil is composed of), a good proportion of it, with some bones broken up and well mixed with the soil for a foot deep. This should cover a space well exposed to the sun ; and this space, be it what it may, should not be shaded by trees or shrubs. Grass lawns will not much prevent the sunshine, and I am fully convinced that a gravel drive in front of a vinery is not an impediment to the success of vines, but, on the contrary, beneficial, because gravel wards off the wet and attracts the rays of the sun in a manner altogether different from mere garden soil.

If such a method is employed in connection with the ramifying roots of vines after the soil has been prepared according to the above directions, and the gravel well rolled, it will form a most beneficial medium for conducting heat to the roots.   Of course there may be a border of, say, six or eight feet, immediately in front of the house and from the main stems of the vines; although I once had a vinery which produced fine healthy crops of fruit where no such border existed and with nothing in front of it but a broad gravel walk and a lawn.   The direct influence of the sun upon the roots of the vine  is no doubt one (if not the chief) cause of their doing well and producing good sound wood with fine coloured fruit free from dis-ease; hence the advantage of my vine-border or pro-tector.   (See illustration.)

On examination we find that all creeping or climb-ing plants live near to the surface of the ground, *i.e.* the roots run under the surface not many inches deep, and the vine is one of these.   Let this fact suffice. The vine border should be fairly drained, but the vine should have some sure means of getting a sufficient supply of liquid food, and this should be of a nutritious character.   Now cow-dung worked into the soil will supply this by being surrounded with the water which the rains give, this being more retentive of moisture than stable manure.   Again, if vines are watered once or twice, during the early spring and summer, with cow-dung diluted with water so as to form a liquid, it will prove a source of great benefit to them.   I am of opinion that guano proves a frequent cause of mildew.

The planting of the vine inside the house has elicited many advocates, with volumes of arguments both for and against it.   In some cases it succeeds, and in some it does not; but I have known only one or two really good instances of success by planting inside the house, while I have known several failures.

Now, some may ask, what difference is there between planting vines inside a vinery, and covering the outside border with glass as I recommend in my 'protector'? A great deal, is my reply; and, first of all, a deeply prepared bed must of necessity be made, consisting of a rich fatty matter, or rather it is so generally, which I can prove is not necessary, for the vine, like all fast creepers and climbers, does not run deep into the soil unless the roots cannot otherwise get the nourishment which they prefer; and if they are compelled to go deep for it, the result is a defect in the state of the fibre; hence so many failures. Secondly, no direct rays of the sun can get at the roots, nor any fertilising air to harden and solidify those channels attached to the stem which are necessary for the present and future health and longevity of the vine. I am able to prove this by a multitude of facts within my own experience, extending over a period of forty years. It is unquestionably the effect of the sun and air playing directly upon the roots of vines that develops a healthy state in them, and when these organs are in a healthy state the branches will be so too. As I have already said, and also proved, when the roots are buried deep in a mass of rich and fatty matter, where no direct rays of the sun can come to them, they will be spongy instead of solid, clean, and firm. Thirdly, no proper method of applying or regulating the necessary supply of liquid moisture to the roots according to their wants can be adopted.

But when vines are planted so that their roots can run outside into soil prepared as I have described, they get both sun and air and moisture as they require it. Then the 'protector' will form the desideratum for regulating the superfluous moisture during the winter, and possesses the advantage that it can be removed when the spring comes, so that the roots can get all the benefits arising from the full play of all three elements.   Here then can be seen the difference between planting vines inside the house and preventing the roots getting outside by walls.   I have known several failures of young vineries caused solely through this, and where they do not immediately fail, it is by reason of a great deal of labour in watering and artificial manure, or else failure would prove inevitable.   Those who intend planting vineries for forcing houses should plant them inside the houses, or rather, let the stems be inside of the front wall and the roots outside.   This is easily done by small arches turned in the front wall under the surface of the bed outside.

### WINTER PRUNING THE VINE.

The manner of pruning the vine depends chiefly upon the constitution of the plant.   Some prune on the long-spur and some upon the short-spur, whilst others do so on the long-rod plan, and each of these may be equally good.   The long-rod pruning can only be adopted when the vines are very strong, and it is known that this method can be safely employed annually without deterioration, or ultimately causing a failure of the vines.

Either of the two former methods may be adopted annually, and some experienced gardeners always prune on the short-spur and get good crops while others adopt the long-spur with similar results. But the secret of success in both cases lies in the strength of the vines, and the management of them during the formation of the young wood the preceding summer.

In some cases close cutting the spur or the young wood to one eye will, to some extent, prove a loss as regards fruit the following season. This will happen in cases where the vines are too thick, and where, during the previous summer, there was an insufficient supply of light and air for the young and early growth, and where the laterals were stopped too soon. The

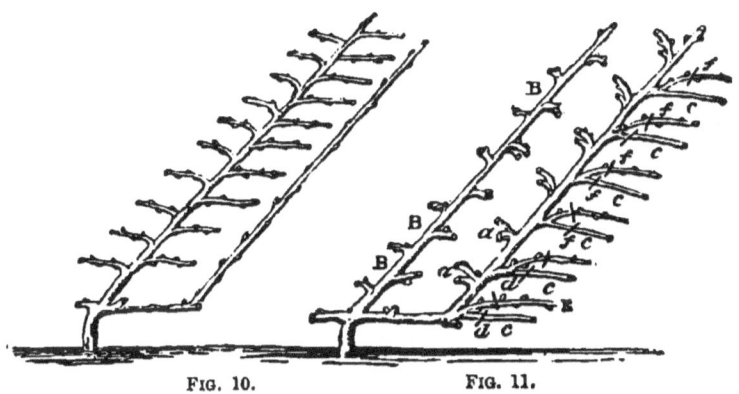

FIG. 10.  FIG. 11.

SECTION OF GRAPE VINES, WINTER AND SUMMER PRUNED.

References to vines.—No. 10, alternate long-rod pruning. No. 11, long-spur pruning, *a a*; B B, rod short-spur pruning; *c c*, laterals that have borne fruit, to be cut at *d*; E, successional lateral to *c*, to be cut off at line *f*.

cause of failure in such cases arises from the imperfect development of the bud or eye. The long-spur method is attended with more certainty as regards the crop, from the fact that under all circumstances the second and third eyes from the base of the last year's growth are the proper fruit buds; and while the base-bud will give fruit, the others will give finer and a greater number of bunches to each eye.

Now a difficulty will present itself to the novice, in this way. If I prune this lateral, leaving two or three eyes this season, where shall I be next year from the leader? Well, you see, here is a base-eye left. Now, as soon as the fruit is formed, and you have selected the best developed bunch of the two or three upon the second or third eye (and it can be easily distinguished which will be the finest bunch as soon as they are in flower), divest the spur of all after-growth as soon as the flowering is over, and leave none upon the spur but what are really wanted for the following season, and encourage the base-bud growth as much as possible. Do not stop it till it is a foot in length, then this will be just in the same position to give fruit spurs as was the one preceding it and which is bearing fruit, and so it goes on successively year after year. It will always be found that the first bud or eye is less prominent than the one above it, and that the third one will be even more developed than either of the other two. This one and those above it are the best fruit eyes.

The time for pruning the vine is a matter of importance. It may be done as soon as the leaf turns yellow and begins to fall, but no pruning should be done to a vine in a house much after Christmas; while for vines which have to be forced, the pruning must be done before that time. In all vine-pruning the weak spray stuff should be cut out clean, or to one eye if necessary, to reserve that one for a supply of wood for the coming season. Never allow too much young growth to remain on young vines to fruit at one time; judgment must be exercised, and an acquaintance with the constitution of the vine is necessary to understand this. I have known young vines ruined by allowing too much of the preceding year's wood to remain on the leaders. If it is, say, three years old and has made vigorous growth, which is generally the case the first five or six years after planting, not more than three or four feet of young wood should be left to fruit on the leaders at a time, from two years after planting till the vine is five or six years old, or until it has been planted so long; and the laterals must be allowed to bear only one bunch of fruit each up to that age. In these days of advanced horticulture I find vines frequently trained just one half too thick in most houses. The consequence of this is premature or unripe wood, which results in a partial or complete failure of the crops, mildew, &c.

No vine leaders should be trained thicker or closer together than two feet and a half, then the ripening and oxidising influences of the sun and air can get at the young wood and ripen it to perfection. To know when this is the case, examine the cut when the winter pruning is done, and if the wood is matured and as it should be, to ensure a good crop of fruit next season, it will be solid and pithless; but if not properly ripened, it will then be brown in the centre and possess some pith. Always use a keen-edged, thin pruning-knife, and make the cut at right angles, or as nearly so as you can, and cut half an inch above the eye.

*SUMMER PRUNING THE VINE.*

This is frequently done in an indifferent manner, but I am of opinion that success depends more upon the summer than upon the winter pruning; for, if vines are not judiciously handled during the summer growth,

the wood will not mature itself, as I have before re-
marked, and then, let the winter pruning be what it may,
and let it be done ever so well, the results will be
either a partial or an entire failure in what might have
been a prime crop of well-grown fruit.

As soon as the fruit shows itself sufficiently to
select the bunches for ripening, divest the vine of all
the laterals, and stop such as are left on for fruiting,
at one eye above the bunch; but never stop the
leaders till they have advanced to the limits of the
house, nor even then if it can be possibly avoided. It
is bad policy in Grape growing to stop the young wood
too soon, and also to allow it to grow too thick. A vine
should be one leaf thick above the fruit and no more.
This is all that is required for a shade to the fruit, and
no more must be allowed if you want well matured
wood for fruiting next year.

All laterals arising after the first stopping should
be frequently removed, and no young wood allowed to
remain but what is absolutely useful for the ensuing
season for fruiting. It is far better to remove old
leaders after the third season than to let them remain,
and to substitute a new leader. In cases where the
vines are strong a new leader can be well trained inter-
mediately, in two seasons, the whole length of a roof
sixteen or twenty feet upwards. A leader will do this
in one season if the vine is strong; it is not however advisable to allow it to remain the whole length
made in one season, but to cut it back one half at
least, and the next season it may remain the whole
length of the roof, when the old leader may be cut
out clean to the bottom.

*FORCING THE VINE.*

The Grape vine is a subject that will bear a high degree of heat, but to apply it properly requires some little care. In its natural habitats it has the advantage of a progressive heat advancing gradually from 50° to 100°, and even above that temperature. Now if a vine is suddenly introduced from, say, 30° or 40° into a heat of 70° or 80°, the probability is that some of the eyes will prove abortive, some of them will prematurely burst, while others—the less matured ones—will not break at all. In forcing the vine, commence with a temperature of, say, 50° for a week, then raise it 5°, and advance 5° more till it is 75°, and when the berries begin to swell 80° may be maintained during the daytime till the fruit is full grown, when a fall of a few degrees will not matter.

As soon as the berries begin to colour, admit air both day and night, keeping up a temperature of 75° or 80° by day, and one of 55° or 60° by night. The sudden fall of 20° by night will materially promote the colouring of the fruit ; in fact, you cannot colour Grapes well unless the night air as well as the day air is admitted. This brings down the temperature, and the low temperature thickens the juices, which get oxidised by virtue of it playing well round the fruit, through the agency of the fire-heat, thus giving a vitality to it which is constantly supplied and quickened by the heat during the day and night. Many people are afraid of admitting the night air, and think the fruit will get a chill, but it is not so. If the fire-heat is kept up, that is, a good heat, with an abundance

of air both night and day, it will be found the only
sure way of colouring Grapes.

## THINNING OUT THE BERRIES.

There is no doubt that frequently too much of this
is done.  In thinning out the berries care must be
taken so as not to maim the limbs too much, for if this
should happen the bunch will suffer from the check to
the free circulation of the sap to those berries left for
perfection.  I think that some of the defects which
manifest themselves in various ways may be attributed
to this thinning out too much.  There is no doubt
whatever but this is the chief cause why Grapes do not
colour so well as people frequently look for.

There are some circumstances connected with Grape
growing under which too much thinning out of the
berries will conduce very much to a want of colour; for
instance, through injudicious management of the early
forcing of the Grape, an imperfect admission of air or
bad air, insufficient light, an uncongenial state of the
roots, a want of moisture during the perfecting of the
berries, or a want of the sun's influence upon the
border or ground in which the vines are growing, &c.—
where any or all of these circumstances meet together,
combined with too much handling and maiming of the
limbs of the bunch, the result will certainly be defect
in colour, shanking off, &c.

The thinning out of the berries should take place
as soon as they are about the size of a Sweet Pea, not
before, nor much after; and all the thinning out should
be done at once.

Liquid manure may in most cases be given to vines once or twice during the summer, but I am of opinion that the kind to be used is very clearly indicated. I consider that guano is not good, as it may cause mildew. There is nothing better, if so good, as diluted cow-dung or sheep-dung. This should be given to weak vines as soon as they have made enough wood to show the bunch, and if they are strong it may be given to them as soon as the fruit is thinned out. One or two good soakings with this may be given during the advance of the fruit to maturity, but not after it begins to colour. The whole of the ground containing the roots of the vines should be saturated with this liquid manure.

## THE LATE VINERY.

Plate 12 shows the roof of a good late vinery at an angle of 45°, which may or may not be double-glazed ; but for keeping late Grapes through the winter I advise to double-glaze such houses. The advantages are obvious : first, double-glazing prevents condensation of the vapour arising from the warmer air of the interior upon the glass below, and consequently upon the fruit ; and secondly, the double glass maintains a more even temperature, for, by a free circulation of fresh air, and a little fire heat to warm the pipes G, no mildew can settle upon the bunches, nor other ill effects arise from long keeping.

In this case, as in that of the early vinery, the border protector, C, will be quite necessary from November until March, when the glass may be removed

for the summer, at which time the border and roots of
the vines will get all the genial influences of the
summer rains and oxidising influences of the air,
which is of some importance, though little is thought
about this matter. This is one of the chief causes why
vines planted outside and where the ground is acted
upon by the full rays of the sun thrive so much better
than they do inside. As I have said before, the full
influence of the sun upon the roots is as essential for

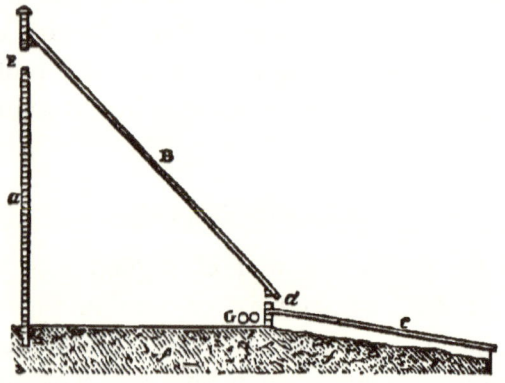

FIG. 12.—SECTION OF LATE VINERY, FACING WEST, AT AN ANGLE OF 45°.

Reference to plan.—a, the back wall ; B, the roof ; c, the border protector ; d, the
    openings along the front to admit air (these consist of my sliding shutters) ; E,
    the ventilation of same sliding shutters as the front, but larger ; ff, the vine
    border and ground prepared under the house ; G, one flow-and-return hot-water
    pipe.

the well-being of the vine as it is for the branches ; in
other words the warmth of the sun for the ground
where the roots are is absolutely necessary, and when
planted inside the house it can never come to them
well. I have seen and have before mentioned the good
effects of the sun's influence upon the roots of the
vine.

The late vinery should be provided with means of
applying heat when it is wanted, for sometimes our

summer weather, and generally the autumn weather, is so uncongenial that in some parts it is doubtful if a crop of late Grapes can be ripened without some artificial means; and almost invariably a little fire is necessary from the month of November till they are cut, to prevent black mildew and to preserve the fruit sweet.

The thinning-out, summer and winter pruning, &c., are the same as for other vineries.

# CHAPTER III.

THIS is a convenient and pretty method of growing·
Grapes. It is a charming sight to see a pot of Grapes
on the table actually growing, when the leaf is healthy,
and the fruit is in its prime with all the beautiful
bloom upon it.

The Grape will accommodate itself to all persons
who possess glass of any kind for growing it in pots, *i.e.*
it can be so grown in any kind of hot-house, cold-house,
or frame. The well-known Mr. Thomas Rivers experi-
mented on Grape-growing many years ago, and found
that it could be done in comparatively small pots for
many successive years, and be made to bear fine fruit.
The difference between getting Grapes early and late
depends upon what sort of treatment they receive.

The Grape seems to flourish for successive years by
annual forcing, provided that the roots can obtain the
nutriment required by the fruit and branches. This
may be effected by weekly waterings with strong liquid
manure, and this may consist of diluted sheep-dung
or cow-dung, which latter is, I think, the best for
vines. Do not give it too strong, but often. One-year-
old well-grown vines thoroughly ripened may be used,
but two-year-old plants are better. The pots may be

ten, eleven, or thirteen inch; but the ten or eleven inch are large enough for three or four years.

The vine must be well established in the pot by the mouth of October, and about the end of November it may be cut back to, say, three feet, and tied to a stick fixed in the pot and may then be set in the house where there is but little or no fire heat, for a week or two.

I find that if vines in pots are pruned and at once placed in much heat they will bleed. Of course all depends upon the state of the roots; if they are at all in an active state—which they frequently are when grown in pots—they will bleed if introduced into a brisk heat immediately after pruning. In the course of a fortnight from the introduction of the vines into the forcing house the heat may be raised ten degrees, and so continue till the temperature rises to 70°, where it may stand until the fruit shows.

When the fruit is fairly set, a few degrees more may be added to the temperature to swell off the berries quickly. No more young wood must be allowed on these vines than is absolutely necessary, that is, only just the quantity of wood which bears the fruit, and as many laterals springing from the base of the spur as will be required for fruiting next year. If only one bunch is allowed on each lateral, the second bud from the base will be a plump one for fruiting next season, but some care is necessary to maintain a good and vigorous habit in these pot-vines by weekly waterings with liquid manure as soon as the fruit is set. The spur system of pruning must be adhered to.

The pots should be set on beds of soil or tan and allowed to remain there till after fruiting, or till the fruit is ripe.    Then the roots will get through the bottom of the pot and feed the vine from the bed.

### *VARIETIES OF THE VINE BEST SUITED FOR POTS.*

Almost any kind of Grape may be grown in pots, but the Black Prince, Black Hamburgh, Royal Muscadine, Chaptal, the Frontignans, Fontainebleau, and the Sweet-water, are all excellent sorts for ordinary pot-culture. These may be had in good strong fruiting canes in pots at 3s. 6d. to 5s. each, and if the wood is well ripened in the autumn they may be pruned at once, carefully shifted, ball entire, into ten or eleven-inch pots and put into the house in the beginning of December, according to the time when the fruit is wanted.

There is a particular advantage attached to the growing of Grapes in pots beyond any other way, viz. that a house can be partly or wholly filled with such vines, which may be increased in number in succession. Some may also be forced very early, and others intro-duced very late, to give a succession of fresh ripened Grapes, which, in my opinion, are far better than those thick-skinned imported ones which possess a covering like thin leather, and have but a poor quantity of juice and that of a very indifferent quality.

Let anyone with a keen palate test the difference between a nicely ripened bunch of fresh Grapes just come to maturity, and one of the same sort which has been hanging for two or three months after the fruit has ripened, and I venture to say that the preference will be given to the more recently ripened.

## THE MARKETING OF GRAPES.

The best way of sending Grapes to market is a matter which often causes some anxiety. It is of the utmost importance to the vendor of fruit that what he sends to the seller is thoroughly well packed, so that no fault can be found, which, by-the-bye, is frequently done with a view to get the lot at a cheaper rate, and sometimes to get it for nothing. I have experienced some of these dodges, and would like to caution the reader against them if he has any fruit to send to market.

As regards sending home-grown grapes to market so as to present them with as much of the bloom on them as it is possible to do, take baskets holding, say, not more than twenty pounds each. These may or may not contain cross-handles ; but I think handles afford a facility for carrying, as then one person can carry one basket without much strain. The fruit being ready, take the baskets into the vinery in the afternoon, when the fruit will be dry, and having a nice lot of perfectly dry lawn-mowings of rather a long growth (say 5 or 6 inches) which have been made in the sun some time before put some of it all round the sides of the baskets to form a padding. Then place some packing or tissue-paper on the hay, and turn the basket on one end, a little slanting. Then let a second man cut the bunches and bring them to the one holding the basket ; place each bunch endways, i.e. the stalks of each bunch uppermost placing the bunches as close together as they can possibly lie, and continue to do so till each basket is nearly filled, and when near the top let the basket gently down on the bottom and fill up with a few more bunches. Then place a few layers of soft tissue-paper over the whole, and on this some thin clean calico, and sew it all round the baskets, straining the calico quite tight. Mark the exact weight of each lot of fruit on the calico cover in ink, so that it cannot be obliterated, and label each basket to its destination, marked 'Perishable goods; with care.'

In the case of Peaches, it is a good plan either to have small fine made baskets or boxes holding a dozen each, placing some fine tissue-paper, cotton-wool, or wadding as we call it, next the sides; then wrap each fruit in a double thickness of tissue-paper, and place them quite close to each other, but not so as to press them too tightly together. Put some layers of tissue-paper or cotton-wool on the top of each small package, and then place from six to twelve of these into a square box or basket made expressly to hold the quantity, fitted with a cover. Mark and label them as for Grapes.

# PART II.

## ORCHARD HOUSES AND GLASS HOUSES.

## CHAPTER I.

### THE CHEAPEST WAY TO BUILD.

THE well-known Mr. T. Rivers was remarkable for constructing cheap orchard houses; but whether that celebrated orchardist was dependent upon the builder, or whether the cost of materials is less now than it used to be, I cannot say; but I am convinced that houses of the same dimensions can be erected at the present time at a considerably less figure. The illustration on next page shows the arrangement of a good Peach-house or a late or medium vinery. If there is a back wall of brick, so much the better; if not, one may be built according to my plan (fig. 5) at the small cost of about 8*l*. for bricks, mortar, and labour, or perhaps a little less. The other expenses of building such a house may be fairly put at 22*l*. 12*s*., which includes the back wall on my plan. Should no wall be required, then a saving of 8*l*. will have to be deducted from this sum. My estimate for such a house includes all the best materials, and painting the woodwork with three coats of anti-corrosive stone-coloured paint, a door at one end, and the other end close-boarded with one-inch boards, ploughed and tongued, or raps nailed on to the joints.

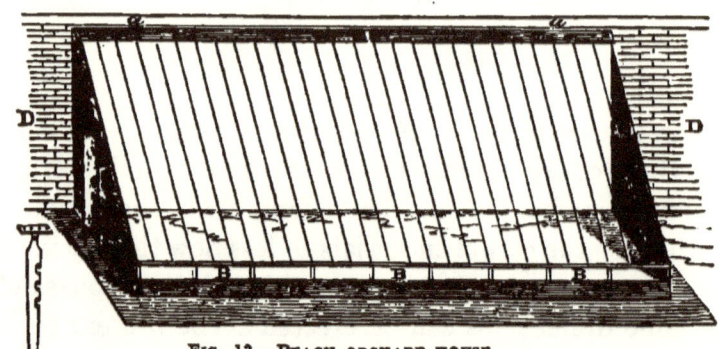

FIG. 13.—PEACH ORCHARD HOUSE,
Top-gearing            Scale $\frac{1}{16}$ inch to 1 foot.
for ventilators.

References.—*a*, flap ventilator; B, ditto shutter one foot wide all along front; *c*, close boarding; D D, the back wall.

Forty feet long, eight feet wide, twelve feet high at back, two feet high in front; to be glazed without putty. Rafters to be eighteen inches apart, and two inches by three inches scantling; glazed with my clips with twenty-one ounce glass, eighteen inches by twenty. The front posts three feet six inches long, three by four and a half scantling. The plates at the eaves, three by four and a half feet; the wall plate, two and a half by three; the board for ventilators, &c., three-quarters of an inch thick. The ventilators to be in ten-feet lengths, hinged with tees; one set of gearing to each ten-feet length.

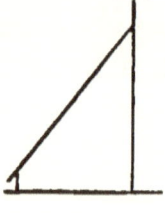

END SECTION.

Such a house can be profitably utilised, and I will now proceed to show how it may be done. The back wall can be planted with oblique cordon Peaches two feet apart. These cordon trees are the best class of wall tree for Peach, Nectarine, and Apricot cultivation as well as for Plums. My reason for saying so is two-fold: first of all, a wall can be covered with these much sooner than by any other kind of tree; and secondly, these trees can be easily lifted once a year to check the over-luxuriant growth which Peaches are so much liable to when in good ground and while they are young. Thirdly, more fruit can be had from a given space than by any other class of tree.

In addition to these trees on the back wall, one row of dwarf pot Plums or Greengages may be set in a line three feet from the wall about two feet apart in the line, that will allow for twenty trees; and in front of these, three rows of pot Strawberries, forty pots in each row equal to 120 pots.

The Plums can all be removed from the house as soon as the fruit is set and placed outside to ripen. The fruit would be set about May, or by the beginning of June, so that no shading to hurt the Peaches could occur, and the whole of the Strawberries would be ripe by that time, so that all these might likewise be removed. Now there will be nothing in this house but the Peaches, which must have air admitted night and day, above and below, from the end of June until the fruit is ripe. The probable result of all this will be a remunerative one.

I may now venture to give some idea of what will be the effect of the careful management of such a house. Twenty Peach trees planted at the back will in the course of two years from the planting, if well managed, give two dozen good fruit each, which at, say, 6s. per dozen = 12l.; 120 pots of Strawberries, each giving annually two ounces of ripe fruit in May, at 6*d*. per ounce = 6*l*. ; twenty pot Plums, each giving, from the second year onwards, three dozen fruit or more, at 3*s*. per dozen = say 11*l*.; total amount 29*l*. from this house, which cannot be considered an over-estimate.

It appears then that within two years from the planting and building of the house the nett cost of it can be realised from its produce, and instead of the profits being less, they will be decidedly more every year afterwards.

Such a house can be most advantageously used for late Grapes, which would in the course of two years, or at most the third season, produce a remunerative crop of fruit, besides which the floor could be used for other things.

### THE PEACH AND GRAPE HOUSE COMBINED.

I am convinced that the same form of house, with a 12-inch high front wall of brick and a row of the sliding shutters such as I have recommended for the early forcing house, can be used for a medium crop of Grapes and early Peaches, by a small heating apparatus and a set of 3-inch pipes running once through the front of the house, *i.e.* one flow-and-return pipe lying on the floor. This apparatus would cost about 10*l*., including the fixing, and the advantages of it would be very great, for the Peaches would be much earlier, and of course of more value. And although the vines could not be allowed to cover the roof, nor be closer than five feet apart, with only one fruiting rod allowed to each vine, yet the crops would be nearly as valuable as a whole one, coming in as they would some weeks earlier. The Strawberries would also ripen the sooner.

## THE OPEN-WALL PEACH PROTECTOR.

This is no doubt the most economical form of glass that can possibly be used for protecting Peach trees on

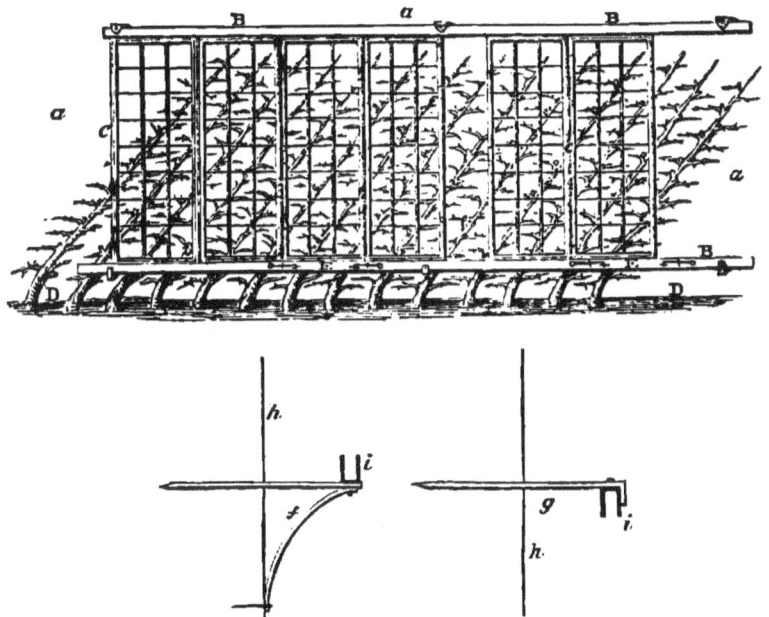

FIG. 14.—SECTION OF PEACH AND WALL-FRUIT PROTECTOR.

References.—*a a*, the wall; B B B, the runs for sashes; *c c*, the sashes; D D, the cordon Peach trees, trained obliquely, and winter pruned; E E, parts of the bottom runs, made to open; *f*, bottom wall bracket; *g*, the top wall hook; *h h*, the wall; *i i*, end section of the runs.

open walls. These movable sashes cost comparatively little, including everything. Each light of ten feet long and four feet wide can be made for 1 *l*. complete and glazed with 21-ounce sheet glass. This will be at the rate of

5s. per foot run, that is, at half the advertised prices. No top coping of glass is required ; in fact, such things are useless, and I may say they are positively detrimental on account of the dryness they cause to the border about the trees and the want of ventilation at the top. It is essentially necessary to obviate any close confinement at the top for wall-Peaches, especially from the time the trees are in flower. Those who recommend the close glazed top coping lights are no gardeners.

These sashes require nothing more than a board ventilator at the top, made to open and shut *ad libitum* by cords fixed on the outside and running through a pulley fixed in the wall, with the cord passing through the run at the top so as to come to the outside in front of the lights. Then the ventilators can be opened and shut without opening the sashes, and the bottom being always open, a free circulation of air is secured at all times—a thing of immense importance in all Peach and Plum growing. The runs are of 1-inch yellow deal for the bottom, with the top cap fixed on iron wall-brackets as is shown in fig. 14. The sides may be of three-quarter stuff, the inner sides of the bottom run being made a fixture, merely nailed on to the bottom ; but the outer side of it must be made to open at distances of 4 feet, to allow of the lights being taken out when required. These openings must be hinged on the bottom and held in position by a couple of staples and a hook. The top run may be a complete fixture.

If the ends of the sashes and the runs are made quite smooth no rollers will be required, as a little grease rubbed now and then in the bottom run will render it quite easy for anyone to push the sashes along without rollers. Moreover, I am not quite sure that the rollers would not offer an easy means for the winds to move the sashes when it would be undesirable. One wall bracket in four feet at the bottom will be enough, and one wall-hook within the same distance at the top will be enough with one screw on the top, and one in the outside, and but one screw in the bottom with the head countersunk and placed inside in the middle of the run.

The sashes need not be opened if the ventilators at the top are opened every morning at nine o'clock during the flowering and setting of the fruit if the wind is cutting and cold, but they should be opened in the mild weather during the flowering of the trees. These sashes are very portable, being made light, and can be utilised for other purposes besides the protection of Peaches or Plums on the walls during the months of February, March, and April, for they may then, if necessary, be taken down, and laid on pits or frames for ridge Cucumber or late Melon growing, or used as screens on frames or pits for such plant-growing as Primulas, Cinerarias, or seedling Calceolarias; the propagation of Geraniums, Cyclamens, &c., for they will not be required for the trees before February. Of course they may be continued on the wall till the Peaches are ripe, which would bring them on earlier and would be equal in effect to the cool orchard house. I know that Grapes can be produced nearly as early behind these sashes as they can be had in a late vinery, *i.e.* one without artificial heat.

Forty feet run of these sashes will not cost more, runs and all, than 12*l.*, and this, with only the difference of the back wall, can be substituted for a cool orchard house that cost 22*l*. 12*s*. The advantages are not quite equal, but that the results will be nearly so I can vouch for, and further I can give plans and estimates in detail for each amount. The bottom runs can be easily taken off by unscrewing them, when the trees require to be lifted.

# CHAPTER II.

## THE PLANTING AND MANAGEMENT OF PEACHES, PLUMS, ETC.

### THE PEACH HOUSE.

ALTHOUGH I beg to refer the reader to my 'Tree Pruner' for full particulars of their pruning and training, yet I feel bound to give some directions in this work as to when and how to plant Peaches and Plums, just as a sort of ready reference.

The best time to plant these trees is, no doubt, from the middle or end of October, or the beginning of November, and to prune them during February and March, for open walls; but for houses the pruning should be done much sooner. In planting Peaches and Plums a full south border should be selected; the soil should consist of a somewhat sandy loam with chalk and some gravel in it; this is necessary for all stone fruits, but especially for Plums and Cherries. A soil that is totally deficient of any of these is scarcely fit for growing any sort of stone fruit. If the natural state of the land is lacking in any of these ingredients, and the subsoil is a cold clay, one of two things must be done, namely, either the border on which the trees grow, and for five or six feet direct from the wall, must be made as described, and raised fully one foot above the common level of the place, or the growing of Peaches, Plums, and Cherries must be abandoned.

In digging the borders on which Peaches and Plums are grown, great caution is necessary above all things. I find on visiting gardens where these fruits are grown, or rather are attempted to be grown, that comparatively young trees are actually killed through the unthinking and ruthless deep digging of the borders with the spade; even Celery trenches are made, and Celery grown of a great size on these borders. I know that there is a great temptation for the gardener who has a small garden to deal with, to appropriate the best and most favourable aspects, so that fine and early Celery can be had; but if he wishes to preserve his Peaches and Cherry trees in first-class health for the full complement of the years they may continue so, he must abandon all deep digging with the spade about these borders. Properly speaking, the borders should never be dug with the spade, nor with the fork, above seven or eight inches—merely prick the surface over only a few inches deep. It is not needful immediately about the stem of Peach trees, nor should be done.

The depth indicated is also quite enough for Radish and Potato growing. Fresh maiden loam and leaf-mould are far better to manure or replenish the Peach border with, than horse-dung. Leaf-mould will grow Radishes, Potatoes, Tomatoes, and French Beans quite equal to, or even better than, stable manure. If the ground gets too poor for the trees, which may be seen by the smallness of the fruit and the weakness of the wood, give one or two good waterings during the summer with liquid manure. One plant of the Tomato may be grown between every two fan-trained trees, but it must be kept from covering the branches and the stems of them.

## THE PLUM HOUSE.

It is evident on all sides that Plums require quite as much protection while they are in bloom as Peaches,

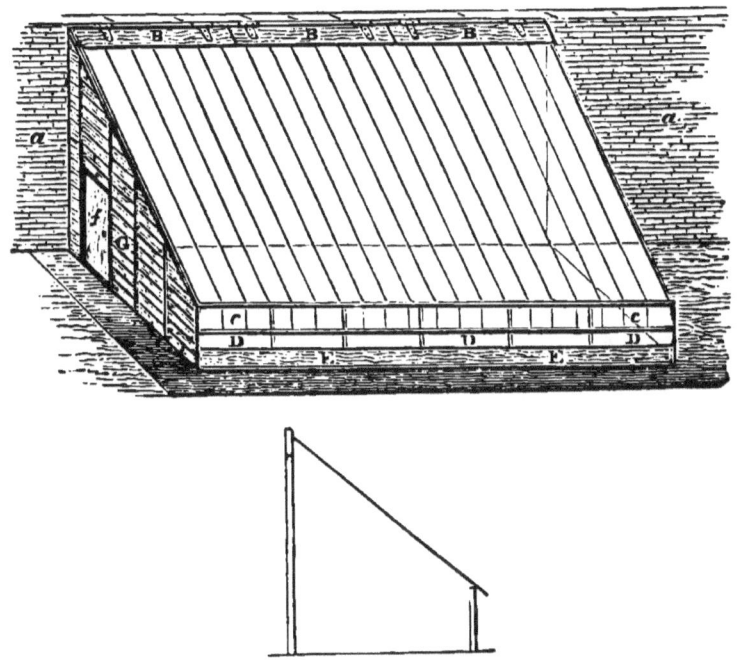

END SECTION OF HOUSE.

FIG. 15.—SECTION OF THE FORTY-FEET PLUM ORCHARD HOUSE.

To be glazed with clips without putty.

Scale $\frac{1}{16}$ inch to 1 foot.

References to plan.—*a a*, wall ; B B, top ventilators, one foot wide, made to open and shut by rack gearing, the same as for fig. 12 ; *c c*, one eighteen-inch row of squares along the whole front, permanently glazed into the wood, and not to open ; D D D, one-foot-wide openings all along the front, with a flap shutter hinged below, and fastened at top with buttons ; E E, eighteen-inch close board ; *f*, the door ; G, the ends, weather-boarded.

but they do not altogether like a close and confined air ; what is wanted is a fair shelter from the cutting winds in the spring when they are in flower. We do not get a crop of Plums of the choice kinds once in five seasons in the open air ; one may be had sometimes on a very favourable wall where the soil is of a warm and dry nature, and the blossom is so sheltered that no cutting spring winds can get at the trees. As to Greengages, the best of Plums, what should we do if we did not get them from France and other countries ? Why, few persons would be able to get them at all, and even now they are too dear for three-fourths of the public to purchase them.

Of all the common fruits the Greengage is no doubt both the most delicious and most useful, yet in many cases it can scarcely be had for money. Few indeed can afford to give 2s. to 3s. per dozen for them, and so they never taste them. This is a pity in a land where there are the means for growing them. I feel determined to induce, if possible, more persons to put up glass at a cheap rate so as to grow such a useful fruit. The cost is but once, and numbers could grow their own Plums and Peaches who now think such a thing quite out of their reach.

More able men than the writer have said and done a great deal to promote Plum growing in this country, and too much can scarcely be written in favour of the art of growing stone fruits, especially the Greengage, Plum, and the Cherry, in our own country, and in a manner that may defy foreign competition. Why should we allow the foreigner to come and take away our business and our credit? We are good gardeners, quite as good as the French or the Dutch. The French have a climate infinitely more advantageous to horticulture than we possess ; and though we are as good gardeners as they are, we suffer through the want of means and other facilities which they possess in this respect. Let our horticultural community then double their diligence and erect glass houses adapted to the various purposes of growing Plums, early Cherries, &c.

The estimated cost of the above Plum house is about 20*l.* Its length is the same as that shown in illustration No. 12, but the width is more, and the front is higher. The back is also higher, with a row of front glass which is not movable. No back is accounted for in this house. The height may seem too much, but it gives a fine chance for the cordon Plums on the same principle as Peach trees are trained. This is really the only way that Plums can be kept bearing when planted in the ground.

This house affords an abundance of head room for good sized pot-Plums on the floor. Twenty cordon Plums may be put on the back, and sixty may be set on the floor in three rows. The floor must be of garden soil mixed with some gravel of a fine kind.

You cannot induce Plums to bear well and constantly every successive season unless they are either planted in gravelly soil or are lifted once a year. What is called 'starving' the trees is the only way of making them bear well every season. Hence pot-Plums will bear much better than when the same sorts are planted in the ground. Almost always and, I might say, invariably, Plums cease bearing after doing so for two or three seasons. Then they begin to make fruitless wood, and you may coax them as much as you like, but if the soil, and especially the subsoil, is not a thoroughly gravelly one, and you do not lift them, they will not bear at all. The result of a house planted on the same plan as for Peaches, and treated in the same manner—

E

except that Plums bear on the old wood and Peaches on the young wood, *i.e.* on the wood made the preceding year—will be a good and abundant crop on the back wall, and also from the pot-plants.

I may venture to make a calculation with respect to the results, for the satisfaction of those who may be somewhat diffident as to whether it would pay to erect such a house merely for Plum growing. In the first place, the actual cost of such a house may be given at 20*l.*, not more. Then there are the twenty cordon Plums at 1*s.* 6*d.* each = 30*s.* ; then sixty dwarf bush Plums for potting at 1*s.* 6*d.* = 4*l.* 10s. ; and sixty eleven-inch pots at 3*s.* 6*d.* per dozen = 17*s.* 6*d.* ; one load of maiden loam and rotten manure, 5*s.* ; total cost, 27*l.* 2*s.* 6*d.* The first year, nothing. The second year, half a crop, say two dozen fruit from each tree at 2*s.* per dozen, that would be, from eighty trees, 160 dozen fruit, which, at 2*s.* per dozen supposing them to be Greengages = 16*l.* The third season, three dozen or more may be had from each tree, till at last four or five dozen fruit may be had in this way. Thus it will be seen that from such a house full 40*l.* worth of fruit may be had eventually, which cost originally, with its contents, but 27*l.* 2*s.* 6*d.* And I do not overrate the thing ; for something more may be made from this house besides the Plums every season.

All the Plums in pots may be removed from the house as soon as the fruit is set and swelled off a little and the danger of frosty nights is over, say by the middle of June. They can then be moved from the house and set upon a good border of soil where they can get all the summer sun, and then the fruit will ripen equally as well as in the house, the floor of which can then be used for show Balsams for seed. The cordon Plums, of course, always remain stationary, but with all the air that it is possible to give them, with frequent syringings. No aphides must be allowed on them, but no syringing should be done after the fruit begins to show. The constant pinching back of the young growth throughout the summer must be done, and the same to the pot-Plums, with a daily watering, and once a week some liquid manure should be given them till the fruit is fully grown, when it may be discontinued.

Now, in a business way, suppose 120 Balsams are seeded in this house from the time the Plums are removed till November, the time they should be re-placed in the house again, at the rate of 2s. worth of seed per plant that would be 12l. in full. Thus it may be seen that a fair living for a small family can be realised from this one house. But let the reader bear in mind that it is easier to calculate these figures than it is to realise the amount.

Let no one, moreover, suppose for a moment that nothing more is to be done than to get the trees and to place them in the house. Some degree of care and trouble is required, including attention to the watering, ventilation, syringing, smoking to kill the aphides &c., a careful lifting of the cordons and replanting them annually while they are young, the constant nipping out of the points of the summer growth, and top-dressing of the pots with a weekly watering of liquid manure during the summer growth, are things not to be omitted. Also ventilation during the growth and flowering in the spring and a daily syringing before the blossom opens—not while it is fully expanded, but immediately after the fruit is set, which may be known by the falling off of the petals. Continue likewise to syringe morning and evening. These are things not to be omitted, or a failure will result, and of course dissatisfaction, and then Plum-growing will fall into disfavour with those who look for great things without trouble.

Many fail, and many try and do not fail, but some few omissions of necessary duties which may not be thought of, or which may be considered of little consequence by the novice, make all the difference as regards results. What a wide range exists in the art of gardening! It is a thing which no one can show by mere writing.

I beg here to refer the reader to my 'Tree Pruner' for all the details of pruning.

## THE CHERRY HOUSE.

The same class of house that is used for Plums may be employed for Cherries, except that more top ventilation may be given, and perhaps more also at the bottom. The top ventilation may be increased from nine inches to eighteen inches in width, and the openings in front may be made double the width of those of the Plum house. The soil should be a gravelly one of a warm nature, but not poor; gravel and sand may exist in land and yet the land be good. If it is not so naturally it must be made so artificially. It would be a difficult thing to do on a very large scale, but for such a place as a Cherry house it would not be difficult.

It is all but useless to attempt to grow Cherries in cold clayey subsoils on a flat surface; I have seen so many failures in Cherry growing that I can do nothing better than speak thus plainly. Cherry trees are very peculiar things to fruit at the rate we might naturally expect, according to the show of flowers they always make. It is often quite amazing to see what an abundance of healthy blossom falls from Cherry trees every spring, and perhaps not one pound of Cherries can be gathered from a tree that would be capable of bearing fifty pounds of ripe fruit did the soil suit it.

Two things seem to be requisite for the Cherry, viz. a warm, dry and free air and a free soil; if the former is low and abounding with moisture, few or no Cherries will be had; if the former condition suits it and the soil does not, the same thing will be the result. I have tried this in my time and have found it to be correct. This brings me to the conclusion that the Cherry likes above all things, and can be best grown under, well ventilated glass. The soil being suitable, and the temperature warm and dry with an abundance of fresh air admitted daily during the expansion of the flowers, the pollen gets distributed and fertilises the flowers more freely than it would do if exposed to the damp of our cold nights, whereby it gets glued and cannot disperse itself, so that the stigma loses its energy. The fruit cannot in consequence stone; hence a partial or total failure arising from such unfavourable atmospheric and subsoil conditions.

Back-wall cordon-trained trees and pot-culture seem to be the proper things for the Cherry. From its peculiar tendency to produce an abundance of flowers one can easily see that it is particularly adapted for close growing either as pot trees or as cordons; what are technically called 'short spurs' are soon formed on it, which will maintain their character as fruit bearers for many years. This characteristic is perhaps more especially a feature of the Cherry than of any other fruit tree ; for when once the spur is formed, and that is quickly done, it will be maintained, I might almost say, as long as the tree shall live. I am referring particularly to the wall or pot-Cherry, and more especially to the ' cordon trained ' tree.

The Cherry is especially adapted for the ' cordon,' more so than any other class of fruit tree ; for when the treble cordon (which I consider the best form for wall Cherries) is planted two feet apart, and trained ' oblique ' against the sun, it may be maintained per-petually for years with much less trouble than in the case of any other fruit tree. ' Treble cordon ' I recom-mend for the Cherry on walls either indoors or out, and trained oblique at an angle of 45° and against the sun. My motive for this will be obvious : all fruit trees, in fact all trees, have a tendency to make more growth towards the sun, and in the case of fruit trees that are trained on walls, we always find that they will make the strongest growth at the extremities; and if these cordon-trained trees, whether Peaches, Plums, Pears or Cherries, are trained with the sun, they will naturally have a greater tendency to make growth at the points, rather than below, on that very account. The sun draws the sap towards itself; but if the tree, whatever it may be, is trained contrary to the course of the sun, then there will be some powerful influence to induce the tree to make growth more regularly over the lower parts of the tree, especially with oblique cordons. Three rods may be allowed to each tree as in the illustration.

If these treble cordons are planted two feet apart, and three rods are allowed to each tree, laid in at six inches apart, they will cover the whole wall much sooner than can be done in any other manner. In the first place, plant strong maidens, cut these back to three eyes at the base; next get three good strong rods and lay them in for permanent cordons the following season. The next season every eye or bud will or should give a shoot, and as soon as these have each made two or three

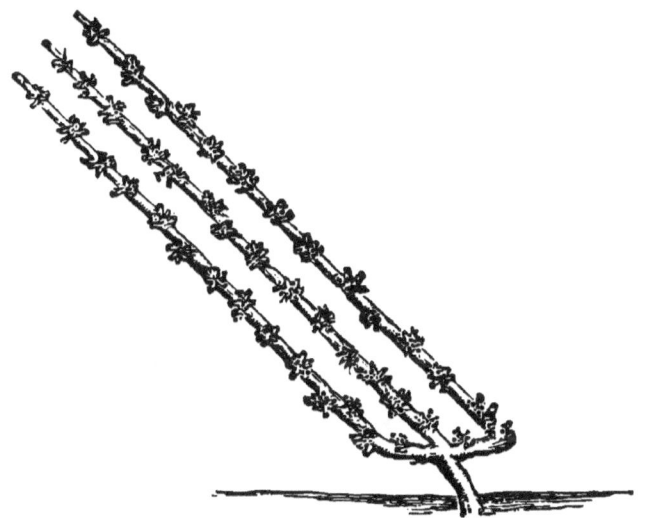

FIG. 16.—TREBLE CORDON OBLIQUE CHERRY, WINTER PRUNED.

inches of growth, nip the point out, thus a fruit-spur will soon be formed corresponding more or less with the illustration above. If there is a tendency in the plants to make more growth at the points of the leaders than should be made, and which would draw too much upon the laterals (which will be seen by the weakness of the latter), nip the points out, this will induce the laterals to make more growth, which is necessary till the spurs are strong, when the leaders may be allowed to advance until the tree is fully developed.

The Cherry above all other fruits is liable to be infested with the black aphides both indoors and out. This pest will so infest the points of the young shoots as completely to stop all further growth, but they will not attack the older foliage. Now the constant nipping out of the points of the young growth will be one means of preventing these attacks. The remedies are, to fumigate them when in the house, and when on the open wall to syringe the trees with some insecticide.

In my opinion a house planted with the May Duke, Bigarreau Napoleon, or the old Bigarreau, each of which bears well, would fetch from 9d. to 1s. per pound freely, for Cherry trees bear abundantly when well managed, and many pounds may be had from one of these treble cordons when it is fully developed. It is seldom, however, that the best dessert Cherry trees can be made to bear on open walls, but under a well-constructed house an abundance of fruit may be had.

Now suppose a house of the same dimensions as the Plum-house with a back wall of the same height, planted with twenty cordon Bigarreau or the May Duke, and trained on this plan, they would cover the wall in the course of four years and be full of fruit-spurs three-fourths of the way up; and on each of these treble cordons there would be in all probability ten pounds of fruit, which at one shilling per pound, ten shillings per tree, 10l., and say 15l. for fruit from the whole of the pot-trees, that would be 25l. from such a house, which would be a remunerative thing considering the little trouble and expense, there being no firing nor pots required after the first outlay. An abundance of air and water, with a daily syringing of the trees as soon as the flowering is over, must be the chief business in Cherry growing under glass. Dwarf bushes for pots may be had at the nurseries for about 1s. 6d. each out of pots, and in pots at 2s. 6d. or so each. So much for Cherry growing. Now I come to what may be called a novel affair.

### THE GOOSEBERRY HOUSE.

Gooseberries can be and are forced in some few lordly places; but as a rule this is new from a commercial point of view. However, I feel convinced not only of

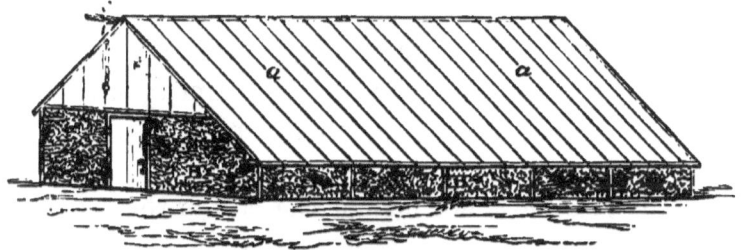

FIG. 17.—SECTION OF A SIXTY-FEET HALF-SPAN ROOF HEDGE GOOSEBERRY HOUSE.

References to house.—*a a*, roof glazed into fixed rafters, twenty inches apart; B B, the walls all round of Yew, Cupressus, or Arborvitæ, and kept clipped; *c*, a section of the ventilator all along the half roof, two feet wide, opened by rack gearing.

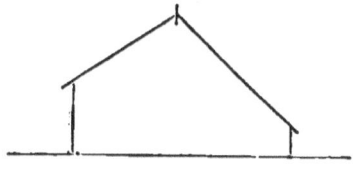

END SECTION OF HOUSE.

its utility, but also of its commercial benefit to the grower. The crop is both a certain and a remunerative one in most cases, and why should it not be so under similar circumstances to that of the Cherry ?

Early Gooseberries are sought after more than any other fruit, and if there is any doubt about getting Gooseberries large enough for tarts by Whitsuntide, with numbers of persons it is quite a serious thing; and then, if they can be had, which is not always certain, as much as 1s. per quart or more must frequently be given. Now an average sized bush will give four or five quarts, and as many as eight or ten may be had from a large bush. Suppose, then, a roughly built orchard house, say, sixty feet long, sixteen feet wide, and seven feet high in the middle, like the sketch above, is appropriated to the growing of Gooseberries, why should it not pay ? The cost of this house will be 27*l.*, everything complete, of good materials, painted with three coats of anti-corrosive paint, glazed with 21-ounce glass, 20 by 18, on my plan, and without putty.

This price does not include the cost of the hedge all round, which would be about 2*l.* 12*s.* for the tree Box two feet high, planted one foot apart, forming a close hedge at once ; 1*l.* 3*s.* for the Arborvitæ, two feet high, planted one foot apart ; and 1*l.* 16*s.* for the common Yew, two feet high, planted one foot six inches apart. But of the three I should recommend the Box, and next to that the Siberian Arborvitæ. The Yew is some time taking hold. These hedge orchard houses are good things for Gooseberry and Plum growing, and if the hedges are kept neatly clipped they look exceedingly well and form a wall nearly as close as a boarded one, so far as observation goes, though they are always open sufficiently to admit a softened air current through the house, so that there is never the danger of suffocating the trees, which is often the case with closed walls of boards or bricks. The outside air passes through these hedge walls in a gradual manner, just enough to meet the demand inside so as to prevent this class of tree from being drawn too much, yet at the same time affording sufficient break and shelter to maintain a temperature much beyond any that can be commanded without glass. Hence it will be found that Gooseberries can be forced and be ready for use several weeks sooner than they would be without glass, and if they are not much in demand before Whitsuntide, they will by that time be as large again as those in the earliest gardens, and of course command a better price if they are grown for sale.

The trees should consist of the early sorts, such as Green Walnut, Jolly Angler, Pitmaston Greengage, &c.; and should be clean-stemmed three-year-old plants; but in no case should anyone buy plants with suckers or spray about the roots or on the stem, for these will be a continual source of annoyance. Gooseberries must at all times, and under all circumstances, be kept free from suckers about the roots, and it should be remembered that it is useless merely to cut them off when they appear, for cutting suckers off close to the ground, or even under the surface, is quite useless. The only way to eradicate them entirely is to take the plant up, and then with the knife cut the suckers clean out from the base, leaving no bud to reproduce them. This should be done whenever they appear.

The trees should be three feet apart, and they may be planted as early as September, but not later than the middle of October; then a crop of fruit may be had the following season. But if they are planted later, little or no good fruit can be expected the first season. They must not be planted too deep, for that is also a cause for the growth of suckers. The roots should be no more than five or six inches under the surface of the ground and well fixed. If the soil is dry, give each tree a can of water as soon as they are all planted. The house should face the south, and the trees should be planted in rows across the house. The pruning may be done at once as soon as they are planted.

The trees must not be excited before January, when the house may be kept closer at the top. The fruit of the Gooseberry is impatient of frost, therefore if it is in danger from the late frosts, mats or *frigidomo* must be laid on the lights at night and kept on for an hour or two after sunrise. If the ground is good, which it should be, the trees will grow strong and produce abundantly. Pruning freely must be resorted to annually—not, however, as some say, by ' pinching out the points of the leaders.' No good gardener will do that except in extreme cases where the leader extends beyond reasonable limits. Let all the leaders grow at full length, except some that are extending too far; these may be merely 'tipped' as we say, *i.e.* cut off a few inches from the points. These main leaders are the future fine fruit-bearers and will produce fruit in long strings.

In pruning, keep the trees well open, and the bodies of them well supplied with some young healthy wood. Cut back the old wood and straggling growth so as to keep a healthy compact growth of fully developed young wood among these house trees. Gooseberry trees will get too large here if not judiciously managed, and if not well managed in the pruning they will be deficient of good fruit-bearing wood.

Liquid manure may be given them from the time the fruit begins to swell till it is ripe ; two ounces of guano to one gallon of water once a week will be found very beneficial. The ground should be watered with this all over, and one good sowing with soot will be found an excellent and stimulating manure for Gooseberries ; this should be put on before the trees break leaf.

Soot is a good preventive against insect pests, especially the fly that produces the ' Gooseberry caterpillar,' a pest frequently very troublesome in the fruiting time. The fly does not like soot, and if it is sown over the whole of the bushes before they break leaf, it will not settle upon them ; soot is also a fine manure for the trees, but the Gooseberry requires a top dressing with some substantial manure besides, which should be put on the ground as soon as the leaves drop, and then forked in with a three-pronged Potato fork (not with the spade), taking care never to dig close to the stem, nor in any case to raise the roots up near the surface of the ground, for be it remembered the Gooseberry will readily emit branches from the roots if they are brought above the surface.

## THE GOOSEBERRY IN POTS.

The Gooseberry will produce a fine and abundant crop of fruit when grown in pots under glass. It is a gross feeder, it is true, but by giving liquid manure to the trees once a week from the time the fruit begins to swell fine fruit may be obtained.

The house illustrated below will be found an excellent one for pot-Gooseberries, and if there is a wall nine or ten feet high, the expense of building such a house will be comparatively small. The back wall can be appropriated either for Plums trained obliquely, or for Red Currants, where they will bear early and abundantly. The Red or White Currant can be trained in exactly the same manner as the Plum or Cherry on the cordon plan. The leaders will remain the same, and will last for years, but all the young growth made the last

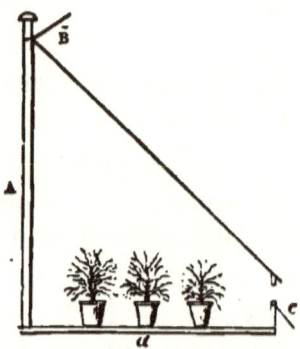

FIG. 18.—END SECTION OF A LEAN-TO HOUSE FOR CORDON PLUMS, OR RED CUR RANTS, ON THE BACK WALL; AND THREE ROWS OF POT-GOOSEBERRIES.

Back wall, ten feet high; front, two feet; eight feet wide.

Reference.—A, the wall, ten feet high; B, the top ventilator, one foot wide all along the house, to open and shut by rack gearing; c, the bottom opening, one foot wide, all along the front of house; d, three rows of pot-gooseberry trees.

season must be cut off close to the spur annually, except such young wood as is required for the filling up of vacant places. (See the 'Tree Pruner.') Greengages will do well in this house if planted two feet apart and trained on the 'oblique cordon plan.'

The above house is set out in the following proportions :—ten feet high at the back, eight feet wide, and of any desired length. The cost of such a structure may be estimated at 4s. per foot run, complete, without the wall, of course. Thus a house sixty feet long would cost 12l. provided that you go first hand to work, otherwise it may cost twice that sum; but even then it might be called cheap by some. But I guarantee that it can be done well and glazed with 15 oz. glass, 20 by 18, on my wind-and-water-tight vertical bar with plain pressure clips. These are far better for glazing without putty than the under clips, i.e. clips which are nailed on cross bars, and then come under the laps, and turn up over the glass; the main difficulty is how to replace a broken square, as no one can replace one from the inside; the whole row must be taken out to put one in at the top or in the middle.

Such a house costing 12l. would hold ninety Gooseberry trees in pots, which, after the fruit is gathered (which would be by May, or perhaps before), might be removed and plunged in the open ground for the summer, kept well watered and encouraged to grow, and the house used for growing ridge Cucumbers or dwarf Beans on the bottom.

# CHAPTER III.

## *THE CUCUMBER HOUSE.*

THIS house will be found the best, and in fact the only safe means for growing winter Cucumbers under the most adverse circumstances. It is almost impossible in the northern counties to keep up enough heat during the winter months under the pressure of sharp and protracted frosts like those which we have experienced the last two years, 1879 and 1880. No ordinary heating apparatus would meet the case in any way adequate to the demand, except by a large amount of extra trouble, such as keeping up a strong fire all night, by attending to it the last thing at night, matting up, &c. ; otherwise some expensive boiler must be used, and even then the severe frost will get in by the morning, or lower the temperature so much that it is almost out of the question in the generality of cases to produce Cucumbers all through the winter ; but by adopting the double glazing, combined with a good ordinary apparatus, and a moderate amount of firing without any late attention, they can be had all through the winter and under all circumstances however trying.

This house (fig. 19,) may be lowered one foot six inches

and the ground excavated, which will be more favourable for winter Cucumber growing than if it were four feet above the surface level; it would then be two feet six inches above the surface, instead of four feet from the eaves to the ground. This house is a roomy one and is especially adapted both for winter and summer use.

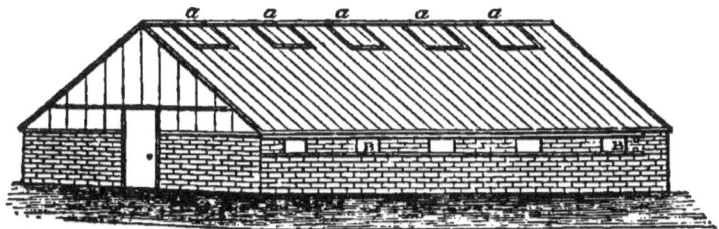

FIG. 19.—SECTION OF A SIXTY-FEET ROSE-FORCING AND CUCUMBER HOUSE.

Fourteen feet wide, four feet high from ground to eaves, ten feet high to the ridge. To be double-glazed on my plan, without putty.

References to house.—a, top ventilators, made to open by rack gearing; B, a set of sliding shutters, two feet by one, along the south side. These work by my cords and pulleys (see figs. 2 and 3).

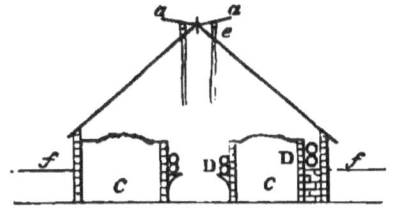

END SECTION OF HOUSE.

References.—c c, pit, four feet wide, four feet deep; D D, hot-water pipes; e, gearing to open lights, a a; f, ground line.

Cost of this house about 54l. 10s.

The winter plants may be grown on the south side, and the summer plants on the north side, there being a pit all round the house which has a south and north roof, which is a great advantage. Moreover it is necessary that a Cucumber house should be adapted all the year round for at least two stages of growth, or rather two

F

crops, without any loss of time, and this house will answer the purpose exactly.

A pit four feet wide should run round three sides of the house, *i.e.* along the two sides, and across the further end from the door. This section of it across the end will be found very useful for forcing Rhubarb and Asparagus, or for plunging pots of forced Roses, Lily-of-the-valley, &c. The side pit on the south will be the best for winter Cucumbers, and the other side will be found the best for the succession of summer Cucumbers. The vines will cover the whole of the roof, or nearly so. It will be seen by the illustration that the pit is so situated as to admit of a pipe running between the wall of the house and the pit to supply the heat at the lowest part of the house on the south side, but none on the north side, where it is not really wanted for summer Cucumbers. But for growing winter Cucumbers a flow-and-return pipe is indispensable.

The pits may be filled with half stable dung and half leaves, which should be well packed and thoroughly mixed, the beds being well trodden in and quite filled. The manure will sink by fermenting.

For this house a good boiler is necessary, such as the thirty-six-inch tubular saddle boiler, *i.e.* thirty-six inches long, which will heat about 450 feet of four-inch pipe well. The price is about 7*l.* Or the improved conical boiler of thirty inches, which will heat about 600 feet of four-inch pipe, the cost of which is 10*l.* This last is a powerful boiler, causing but little trouble, and perhaps the most economical as regards firing and attention, and, in conjunction with the sure and safe circumstances connected with 'double glazing' of such a house, no better or less expensive boiler can be had.

These boilers have two flow outlets, which are necessary for this kind of house, and they also have two returns. The Thames Bank Company, London, keep a large stock of boilers of every class and size, and every kind of connection and fitting. They have also a patent method of fixing the pipes by means of *india-rubber rings* for the sockets, which offers such a facility for fixing hot-water pipes that any ordinarily good workman can fix them. I can fix them myself. I was much pleased with the idea when some little time ago I had an apparatus from them to be attached to a Cucumber house. I will endeavour to give the cost of it, and I find by a pretty correct calculation, that for an efficient apparatus with one of these thirty-six-inch conical boilers, 360 feet four-inch piping, and all necessary connections, together with the fixing, the cost will be 36*l.* as nearly as possible ; but it must be remembered that this is a powerful heating apparatus, and able to keep up a growing heat let the weather be what it may, ordinarily speaking.

The cost of building the house will be about the same as for the early vinery with the border protector, complete, viz. 54*l.* 10*s.* This is at a much lower rate than is usual, more than 50 per cent., and 'double-glazed,' without which no house can be guaranteed frost-proof, or even warranted to maintain a temperature sufficient for Cucumber growing in the winter.

Those who contemplate growing Cucumbers for the winter should get the house finished by July and ready for making the bed by the end of the month, and as soon as August comes, commence to make a good bed in the south pit, and when the heat rises sow the seed.

I prefer seed to plants from cuttings for this winter
work, because seedlings are rather more free of growth
than cuttings.  At intervals of three feet all along
the middle of the bed place a hillock containing
about half a bushel of fine maiden loam and decayed
stable dung of about equal parts, and make each of
them a little flat on the top similar to the bottom of a
basin inverted.  The next morning draw a circle with
the finger on this flat about an inch deep, and place
three seeds in each, and cover them up an inch or so.
In the course of two days and two nights the seedlings
should appear, and will do so if the bottom heat is
good and brisk (which it should be at this time), and if
the house is kept closed.

There will be no danger of scalding if half of the
bed is of leaves raked up last autumn, and kept open
so as not to decay too much.  These old leaves are
fine moderators of the strong fermenting properties of
fresh stable dung.  As soon as the plants are up, shade
them during a hot sun from its full influence for a
week or two till the plants get strong, which shading
must then be discontinued except on some very bright
days.

As soon as the roots of the plants begin to run out
add more soil to each hillock, and finally fill up, making
eight or nine inches in the depth of the soil over the
whole bed.  The compost as a rule should not be sifted,
but merely chopped with the spade, mixing all the
lumps and fine together.  If more than two plants
come up in each hillock, the third may be removed, but
even one is enough for fruiting.  As, however, some
casualty may happen from various causes, it is best not

to be in a hurry to remove the second plant before you can make sure of one good one.

No fire-heat will be necessary before September when the nights begin to get cold, and water must be carefully given at first. A little air may be admitted above, but not much and only on fine days. If insects appear, fumigate immediately. The most troublesome pest is the thrip; no time must be lost as soon as it appears, but apply at once some mild insecticide by carefully sponging the under side of the leaf, or apply tobacco powder with a dredging-box to the same part of the leaf, for this is where it secretes itself, and if left alone for a few days, woe be to the Cucumber plants, for the remedy will very likely be as bad as the disease. So hard is this pest to despatch, that in nine cases out of ten it will be a wonder if you do not kill the plants in trying to despatch this tenacious enemy. Watch therefore and keep up a sharp look-out for its first appearance. There are few other enemies likely to trouble you so much as this in house Cucumber growing.

As soon as the plants reach the roof, which should be provided with wires on which to train the vines, the leaders should be stopped. This will induce the plants to give two or three laterals, which must be trained out, and as soon as these get a foot long stop them, which will induce more laterals, and these will give fruit. As the vines advance some thinning out will be necessary. Do not allow them to become confused, but keep them well trained and moderately thin. At times some cutting back of a portion of the leaders will be necessary to prevent a lack of young stuff, and consequently fruit, at the lower part of the vines.

As the winter draws near, say, November and onwards, a good fire-heat will be necessary. A heat of 75° must be kept up during the day, allowing a fall of 5°, and not more than 10°, at night. Some liquid manure may be given to the plants when they are in bearing, but care is necessary as to what sort is used, and for this purpose I am of opinion that nothing is better than slight dressings with nitrate of soda, with now and then a very slight sprinkling of soot over the surface of the bed. These are of course in powder, and not in a liquid state. Both of them are remarkably strong stimulants and must be used with great care. They are good preventives against the progress of insect pests also. Guano, and animal manures such as cow-dung and sheep droppings, are frequently a source of trouble as well as advantage, for while I admit that they are good stimulants, they also frequently introduce numerous insect plagues into the house or frame, and where such tender plants as the Cucumber or Melon exist, they cause an incalculable amount of trouble.

The pit on the north side of the house can be well and profitably used for forcing Rhubarb from November till March by placing some leaves two feet thick at the bottom, treading them in tight, setting the roots upon the bed with a little soil on them, and then some leaves over the roots. Or cover the pit over the top so as to exclude the light, and an abundance of Rhubarb can be had by the end of December or in January; or, again, a bed may be made by filling the lower part three feet up with leaves only, watering as you proceed, and treading them in tight. Then put nine inches of fine soil on them and make them level; place three- or four-year-old Asparagus plants as close as you can; put

them all over the bed, and cover the whole with four or
five inches of fine and good sandy soil, composed of one
part maiden loam, one part old pulverised manure, and
one part sea sand. The plants may be put on this bed
in November or the beginning of December.

Asparagus thus forced will be early and good and
will pay perhaps better than anything else. At a fair
computation full 20*l.* worth of good saleable Asparagus
may be had from this bed by March if the roots are
strong and good, well bedded in, and watered, as soon as
the heads show up, with salt water. Do not shade them,
and get the heads as green as possible. In bedding the
roots in, first examine every crown and cut out all the
weak buds which are found round the most prominent
ones, as these will give only small spray stuff and will
materially weaken the buds for fine Asparagus.

As soon as the middle or end of March comes it
will no doubt be so far over as not to be worth retain-
ing, therefore remove all the roots, and off with the
soil and one half of the leaves, which will be partially
decayed. Then make up the deficiency with fresh
stable manure, and fork the whole over, turning and
well mixing both the old leaves and the fresh manure
together, making a good firm bed for the summer
Cucumbers. The plants for this batch should be strong
ones struck from cuttings a week or two previous to
making up the bed, and as soon as it has a little
bottom heat, which will be in a day or two, put the
plants out as for the winter batch. It will be necessary
to keep a sharp look-out for the red spider and thrip
at this time. Keep up a nice humid atmosphere
in the house by syringing all the pipes every morning,
and in the evening also during the fine sunny days as

the days draw out. Give top ventilation during hot sunny weather ; shade and close at four o'clock.

*Shading.*—I have found that a green shade of a light nature is a good thing and that a very thin transparent green paint laid on the glass outside for the summer is good for some things. But for Cucumbers I can hardly recommend it ; fine green gauze is as good as anything for shading the sunny side of the roof, but none will be required for the north side. If the gauze is sewn together, with tapes sewn all round the edge, and one across the whole width (*i.e.* the width of the south roof), at distances of three feet, it can then be tacked on the roof and strained quite tight. The shading may remain on during the hot months without any harm.

When the young Cucumber plants begin to bear the old ones should be removed, for they will only engender numerous insect pests. Clear all out, therefore, soil and all, except a few inches to form a surface on which to place pots of Balsams, Cockscombs, young Primulas, &c. I am not disposed to raise the expectations of anyone too high, but I may assert for a fact that by good practical judgment and management such a house can be made to pay more than the cost of erection the first year, but not if you go to professional builders, for then such a house complete will cost fully 50*l*. more, heating apparatus and all. For the satisfaction of some I may venture on an estimate of what may be made from such a house the whole year in and out :—Asparagus, say 20*l*. ; early Cucumbers, say 800 at 1*s*. each, 40*l*. ; late ditto, 800 at 6*d*. each, 20*l*. ; cut Lily-of-the-valley from the pit across the end, say 2,000 spikes, more or less, at 8*l*. per 1,000, 16*l*. ; 300

pot plants, various, at 1s. each, 15l. Now, no one can dispute this, yet it will more than cover the first cost of the building and apparatus complete.

## THE MELON HOUSE.

The same class of house which has been already described for Cucumbers will do well for Melons, except that a flatter roof may be used. An angle of not more than 30° should be employed for Melons, as no shading should be given them. There is a vital difference between growing Melons and Cucumbers. The latter require quite as much heat, but not so much light; and upon the whole the Melon is much easier to grow than the Cucumber, as a rule, to which there are some exceptions, of course, and these relate to the growing of early Melons.

Early Melons are difficult to set as regards the fruit, for want of sun, and the difficulty is much greater when they are grown in frames than when grown in houses. If they are grown in well-ventilated and light houses, much less trouble will arise in the setting of the fruit. In frames they are difficult to set, on account of the close damp air; but in a good house the air is freer and drier, so that the pollen is easier of distribution by insects or otherwise.

For growing early Melons, large sized glass, a flatter roof than is used for Cucumbers, facility for giving air, and no shading—these are the conditions for good success; also never to allow the vines to get thick and confused. Nor does it answer to turn the foliage underside uppermost. Some may not see the importance of all this, but I know from experience that these things are all important in Melon growing, and although the Melon may be regarded as giving less trouble than the Cucumber, yet some few precautions are necessary that are not needed in the case of the Cucumber. For instance, no water should ever be put upon the collar of the plants, *i.e.* round about the stems immediately attached to the roots; Cucumbers do not like too much of that, but Melons will canker or shank off if they are watered there.

The Melon is very liable to the red spider in both houses and frames, but more so in houses, especially when the fruit is ripening. This arises from the dryness of the air; the thrip will also trouble the Melon in its early stages of growth, before the fruit gets half its proper size. The same remedies which have been recommended for the Cucumber may be used here; but if some flour of sulphur is kept in the house, laid on dry slates or sheets of iron where the sun can get at it, and where it will be safe from the wet, sufficiently gentle and harmless fumes as regards vegetation will be given off, which will act as a preventive to the red spider, thrip, &c. As a preventive is far better than a cure, I have no doubt but that this remedy will answer well; but if either the red spider, or the thrip, is allowed to get thoroughly established on the plants, and recourse must be had to strong doses of sulphur fumes to despatch them, nothing can be more dangerous, for very small overdoses of sulphur fumes will destroy every plant. Tobacco fumes are useless to destroy these insect pests.

As soon as the Melon plants reach the roof of the house—which is no great distance, for the top of the

bed should not be above one foot from the lower part
of the roof—they must be trained back a little to reach
the lower rafter before they can be brought forward
up the roof, so that probably two feet will be the distance the plants will have to travel up a stick before
they can be stopped, and this must be done as soon as
the point fairly reaches the rafters. This will cause
them to make two or three shoots, on which probably
fruit may show. If so, nip them off, for no fruit must
be allowed to remain yet, not till the plants have
reached three or four feet up the rafters, then nip out
the points of each leader. This will induce a lateral to
each leaflet below, and on these will be the fruit.

As soon as one fruit on every third lateral has set,
cut all the rest of the laterals off, leaving the one with
the set fruit on it. The setting of the fruit consists
in stripping the petals from a male blossom, leaving
the stamens which contain the pollen. Then take the
female or fruit-bearing flower between the two fingers,
holding it steady, and twirl the anthers containing the
pollen in the stigma, or centre of the blossom, on the
fruit, fix it there, and leave it for fertilisation. This
setting must be done at a suitable time, i.e. when the
flowers are wide open and dry. Allow one of the top
laterals to each leader to remain as a leader to advance
up the roof so as to cover it. Train them in regular
Grape-vine order, keep the vines thin, and by stopping,
an abundant crop of fine Melons will be had all over
the roof.

It is rather difficult to manage Melons in a continuous and successional crop, that is, constantly ripening fruit, with others continually coming on, for those
that are ripening and coming to that state are apt to

crack if much water is given to the plants; at the same time the half-grown fruit requires plenty of water in order to get it fine. It is better to get a batch of fruit all over the house if possible, and to ripen that batch. Cut them, as ripe Melons will keep for some time, and then encourage the vines to make good growth as much as possible by cutting in and giving liquid manure. All the second growth will now be full of fruit, and this crop may be had as fine as the first.

The chief difficulty in Melon growing lies just here: during the ripening of the fruit, the withholding of moisture to get good flavoured fruit gives an advantage to the red spider. My plan was to get a batch as fast as it was possible by keeping up a brisk moist heat till the crop was near perfection, then to give an abundance of air, and very little moisture for a few days till the fruit began to change to a paler colour, and when a strong perfume was given off by the fruit, to cut it, and as soon as ever the batch was cut to stimulate the vines as much as possible, as I have said before; thus the red spider may be partially or wholly avoided.

There are a multitude of sorts now catalogued, and no doubt each has some merit of its own; but in my opinion there is no better Melon than the Golden Perfection. It is of the most exquisite flavour and of a fine medium size. The old Beechwood is another splendid green-fleshed Melon. The latter is a round variety, and the former is a little oval-shaped. I think upon the whole that a round fruit looks better on the table than some of those long Vegetable-marrow-looking sorts. Golden Perfection is not out of the way as regards length, being only slightly oval. Munroe's

Little Heath is a fine ribbed and netted Melon, with scarlet flesh of good quality, and a fine fruiter. Then there are numerous other sorts pretty generally known.

The Water Melon is a large and very delicious variety. It is grown abundantly in Texas, one of the States of America, where Melons grow to perfection without any trouble; the farmers there simply put the seed in the open ground in the cornfields, and they grow up and bear very large fruit, which ripens to perfection, and which the people find of great value during the hot season. I have no doubt but that any of our Melons would grow to perfection there quite as well as the Water Melon; but then they are not required, they say, because the Water Melon is by far the best.

Melon seed is, as a rule, the better for being two or three years old but for house-work I think one year old is the best; for the older seed not having so much vitality in it as the newer, the plants grow less vigorous than those from new seed, which does well enough for frame-work, where as a rule there is sure to be too much vine. But for covering the roof of a house, vigour in the vines is necessary.

### THE MELON IN PITS AND FRAMES.

A pit or frame for Melon growing should not be less than five feet six inches or six feet wide, inside measurement. If narrow pits are used there is not room enough for the proper development of the leaders, and these have to be stopped too soon or allowed to take a retrograde or side course, and thus get so thick and confused that no air can come to the blossom to fertilise the fruit; hence we often find that the fruit drops off when about the size of a filbert.  But when there is sufficient room in the pit or frame, whichever it may be, it will allow of eight main leaders from one plant—and one plant is better than two to each light —running out from the stem in regular divergent order, one to each long point, and one between these, making eight altogether.  These main leaders should reach to their limit before they are stopped, which should be done as soon as they have reached it, when laterals will be emitted at every leaflet along these main leaders, on which will come an abundance of fruit, when as many should be selected for maturity as may be thought fit, and the rest cut off.

All growth in the vines made after the fruit begins to swell should be nipped off, thus keeping the whole plant clear.  In this way an abundant quantity of extra fine Melons both in size and flavour will be ensured.  As a guard against the thrip, place some flour of sulphur upon slates laid on the bottom of a flower-pot turned bottom uppermost so as to rise above the foliage of the plants, and where the sun can play upon the slate, when gentle but sufficient fumes will be constantly emitted so as to be a check to this insect pest.

Air may be given the plants during all sunny weather; but close early, before the sun leaves the frame—one hour before drawing in its life-giving in- fluences.  If these few directions concerning Melon growing are observed, great success will attend you without any serious drawbacks in the shape of insects.

The same routine as regards vapour, watering, &c., as I have already given for house Melons, is applicable here, except that for very early Melons more bottom

heat is necessary in frames and pits than in the house.
For these latter, when grown in pots, it is a good plan
to have one flow-and-return three-inch pipe once round
the pit above the surface, or even a two-inch pipe would
do. Such a thing is very inexpensive: two-inch pipe
costs but 1s. 6d. per foot. That would be 4l. 10s.,
elbows and all, for a pit 30 feet long; and the whole
cost of the boiler and everything would not be more
than 9l., or perhaps 10l., including the fixing. These
surface pipes are very beneficial for early Melon growing in pits.

The bottom heat must arise from a well-made bed
of stable manure and leaves well mixed and well
packed in, forming a tight and compact bed not less
than four feet deep for winter work. It is useless, or all
but useless, to make a bed for early Melons except it is
well made : one half leaves raked up in November, and
one half fresh stable manure, I have found the best
materials for making such a bed. There is no fear of
too strong a heat arising, as is the case when all stable
manure is used, nor do the materials require two or
three weeks' fermentation and turning previous to
making the bed if a proportion of one half leaves is
used. As soon as the heat is up to 60° the seeds or
plants may be inserted.

The angle at which a pit or frame should be constructed for Melon growing may be regulated by the
same principles as for the roof of the house used for
the same purpose. For the first crop of early frame
Melons a bed should be made up by the middle of
January, and if two-inch pipes are used for surface heat,
Melons may be had by the end of April or the beginning of May; but the pipes for the surface heat need

not be used till the fruit is half grown if a good bottom heat exists.

The next best way of cultivating Melons to that of growing them in a good house, as described and illustrated by the plan for Cucumbers, is a pit and tank. There is no doubt but that the tank system is the best and most economical upon the whole, as well as the most effective. Tanks are rather expensive things to construct in the first instance, but are less so in regard to the subsequent attendance and labour. Almost everyone knows most of this, I am aware; but not everyone can tell the cost of constructing such an apparatus, and may imagine it would be even more expensive than it really is to build such a tank.

## THE TANK FOR CUCUMBERS AND MELONS.

The outside brickwork of this pit need not be more than half a brick thick, which of course must be carried down to the bottom of the tank E. The tank must have a separate brick of four-and-a-half-inch work next to the walls of the pit, which must be laid in cement, and the division c must also be laid in cement. The bottom of it, which should be double work, *i.e.* two bricks laid on one another, making six-inch work, should also be laid in cement. The tank must be plastered half an inch thick all over with good Roman cement up to the water line B B, about six inches. The floor D D may be of slate slabs, or stone, or large floor tiles. These can be had of any size by order, I have no doubt; the size need not be extra large.

If the tank is, say, six feet out and out, deduct eighteen inches from that for brickwork, which gives four feet six for the tank itself, and leaves five feet three

inches to be divided into two parts for the floor, because
the floor must butt up to the work of the pit, covering
all the work of the tank. This gives a division of two
feet seven and a half inches for each slate or tile, each
one reaching from the walls of the pit half-way on to
the division C, and lying quite close side by side, no
steam to hurt will get through. The tiles or the slates
should be from one inch to one and a half inch thick.
It is waste of money to make the floor of wood, as the

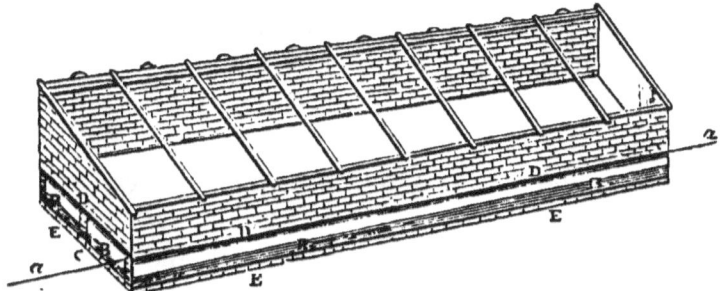

FIG. 20.—THIRTY-FEET SECTION OF A SIXTY-FEET MELON PIT.

References to pit.—*a a*, ground line; B B B B, water in tank; C, brick division running the whole length, for flow and return hot water; D D D, floor on which the
soil rests for the plants.

steam soon destroys it, but the slates or tiles will last
a lifetime with care, *i.e.* if not jumped on, &c.

The tanks, *i.e.* one flow and one return, should be
on a level except a few feet at the cold end approaching
the boiler, which should be on a fall towards it a few
inches but not too much; the boiler is always fixed
considerably below the level of the bottom of the tank,
so that the water flows rapidly into it. If a very rapid
circulation of hot water is required, some fall towards
the boiler from the far end of the return tank is necessary; but remember that the waste of water and the
wear and tear of the tanks is more.

The cost of such a pit may be fairly estimated at
36*l.* more or less, according to the distance the bricks
have to be carried and the other materials, but I have
put the highest possible figure upon everything connected with this pit. I have calculated 1*l.* 10*s.* per 1,000
for the bricks, which would include the carting if not
too far from the kiln. The number of bricks required
for a pit sixty feet long and six feet wide, with single
work for the outside walls, six feet deep at the back,
four feet above ground, and two feet below the surface
all round; with five feet deep for the brickwork in
front; single bricks laid in cement for the sides of the
tank, and brick on edge laid in cement for the bottom
of the tank, will be about 7,849, perhaps a few more
or less. I have allowed 5*l.* for a good boiler, connections and setting—one of those tubular saddle boilers
at 3*l.* 16*s.* will answer the purpose well, and I have also
allowed 12*s.* per sash complete for the frame-lights,
which is ample; 5*l.* for floor tiles for the cover of the
tank, for the soil &c. to rest upon, and 4*l.* or nearly so
for labour alone, which I am sure is ample; so that it
will be found that this estimate is not much out of the
way.

Now let us see what can be done in one year with
it in a commercial way so as to pay the cost. I will
suppose that the pit is completed and dry by September. In the first place, it may be filled with
Rhubarb, of which it would hold 360 very strong roots,
each of which would give at the least two pounds weight
of Rhubarb, and this at 6*d.* per pound will be 18*l.* This
Rhubarb would be all over in time for a second crop of
Melons, which would be as valuable as the first crop.
Supposing that 155 fruit only were got from this whole

pit, at 3s. each = 23l. 5s. for Melons; and then the pit could be used from July until November for bringing on flowering plants, such as Primulas, Cinerarias, &c. without heat ; so that it is plain enough that the cost of such a pit can be repaid by its own capacity within one year.

# CHAPTER IV.

THE Lily-of-the-valley and Christmas Rose, or Helleborus, are more in request in the winter and early
spring than anything else, perhaps, among flowers. The
difficulty of getting the Lily-of-the-valley early, with
the foliage (which is in reality the beauty of a bouquet
or a button-hole) is not small, especially from fresh-
planted roots. It is next to impossible to procure the
foliage and flowers early from fresh roots, even if they
are potted as early as they can be obtained, which is
never before November, because the buds are not
matured sooner than that. If, too, the best 'clumps'
are used, and potted as carefully as you can, and the
pots containing the roots are plunged into the best
possible bottom heat (too much of that however will
not do for these things), yet for all this flowers and
foliage at one and the same time cannot be had from
these fresh-potted roots.

There is no more stubborn plant to force among
flowers, and the only way to succeed in getting both
flowers and foliage early is to have command over the
plantation of roots so as to get both at pleasure. To
this end I have given my view of the only method

likely to meet the desired object. The pit shown below has two distinct aspects and two uses. The Lily being stubborn in its nature to obtain early, should be planted on the south side of this pit ; and the Helleborus, being quite the reverse, should be planted on the north side of it. I propose that this pit should be sixty feet long, and five feet wide inside on each side of it, built with four-and-a-half-inch work throughout ; three feet high at the back from the floor, $h\,h$, to the ridge, and one foot

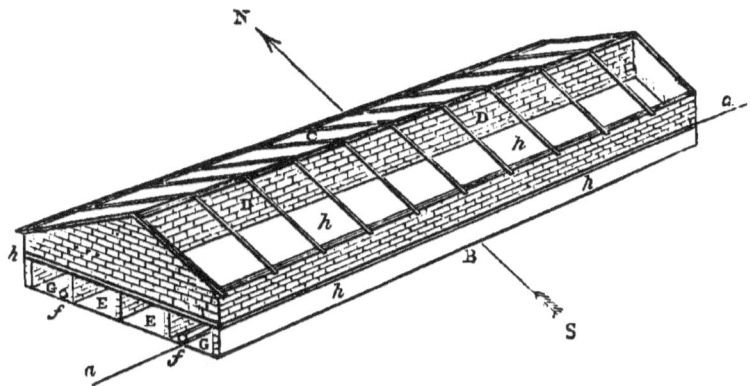

FIG. 21.—FORTY FEET SECTION OF LILY-OF-THE-VALLEY PIT.

References to plan.—$a\,a$, ground line ; B, south aspect ; C, north aspect ; D, middle wall ; E E, underground chambers for heat ; $ff$, partition walls, to be pigeon-holed, to admit of the heat passing from chambers G G to E E ; $h\,h$, slate floor.

six inches in front; the sashes made to slide as is usual, so that they may be taken off and put by for the summer months or used for other purposes, as the Lilies and the Hellebores do not require them on after May. In fact they will be much benefited by full exposure to the influences of the rains and air all through the summer months till November. My object is to make permanent plantations of both the Lily-of-the-valley and the Helleborus niger in the soil, a good bed being placed on the floor *h*, where the roots may remain for years and give flowers annually at an early season, by having one flow and one return three-inch pipe for both pits, that is, the flow pipe to run through the middle of the front pit close to the partition wall *f*, which wall must be pigeon-holed so as to admit of the heat passing to the back of the pit. No other flooring is required beyond the clean firm ground or gravel for the pipes to lie on. One small boiler is all that will be needful to heat these pits, for no high temperature is necessary in this case.

The floor on which the bed is made, and in which the plants are set, may be made of common house-slates of a large size and laid double. If slates of the length required, two feet six inches, cannot be had (although I think they can), oak plank may be used, but slates or paving tiles, as recommended for the Melon pit, are the best. This floor must be quite level, resting on the chamber walls from the front to the middle, coming halfway on to the middle wall; and on it the soil must be put for the bed. This should consist of good maiden loam one part, decayed manure one part, and good pit or river sand one part; not sea sand, nor sand containing mundic or any injurious minerals. The bed should be one foot thick from the floor in front, but more depth may be allowed at the back, thus giving it a slope towards the front; one foot six inches will be ample for the depth of it at the back.

The soil should be chopped fine with the spade, and for the Lilies some fine sifted soil should be placed on the surface in which to insert the plants; but for the Hellebores no finer than what the bed is composed of is necessary. In the month of October the Hellebores should be planted all over the bed one foot apart every way, if strong plants ; and the Lily-of-the-valley should be planted as soon as they can be had, which will not be before the middle of November for mature buds ; and here I recommend single crowns as the best for making the plantation.

The pit of the Lily will take about 2,700 roots, single crowns, at four inches apart, to plant it well. These single crowns should be all matured roots, each with a bud that will give a spike of flower, one or more, the first season, that is, if those are used which are required to flower the following spring; if not, any good roots may be used, which can be had in some localities from our woods, but these may not flower for two or three seasons after planting.

If the single crowns are used that are offered by the trade growers of this plant, such as Krelage or Roozen, of Holland, every one of them will give one or more spikes of flower the following spring, which from a commercial point of view is of much importance to many men, for 3,000 spikes of flower at 16s. per hundred would realise 24l., which would go a long way towards paying the cost of the pit the first season. The cost of the roots would be 5l., but you will never have to buy again.

In planting these single crowns of the Lily, first make the bed moderately fine, and put three or four inches of fine sifted soil comprising a good portion of sand and some fine leaf-mould on the top of all, and rake it over so as to make it close and even all over the surface. Then draw drills across it with a half-moon hoe deep enough to let in the crowns an inch below the surface of the bed, press the roots well into the drills, taking care not to let the fibrous roots turn upwards ; and cover each planted drill as you proceed.

Perhaps for an inexperienced hand it would be the best plan to make the surface fine by raking, then to place the roots all over it four inches apart, and to put the fine sifted soil over the whole, covering the crowns about an inch. After a day or two give the whole a good watering with a heavy rose so as to settle the soil well to the roots, and place the sashes on the frame.

The Hellebores may be planted by means of the spade. There are many varieties of this genus. The real Niger is not so strong-growing as some others, but it is the best, having purer flowers than the common sort. The best are the Chinensis and De Graaf alba. As much depth of soil as the pit will admit of should be given these, that is, nearly up to the glass in front, with one foot six inches at the back, and the crowns must be three or four inches below the surface ; give a good soaking with water after all the roots are in.

Small roots may be had wholesale at 60s. per thousand. The pit for these will take about 300 good roots, and more if they are small. Some will say, why plant Hellebores in frames, since they can be lifted from the ground and forced there and then ? I admit it, but at the same time I know that the sorts I have named are very impatient of frequent removals, and have to be sacrificed for some time after they are lifted from the ground for forcing purposes, and a year or two is thus frequently lost in regard to such roots in this way. But if they can be gently forced where they are perpetually growing, no loss will be sustained.

Neither this nor the Lily-of-the-valley requires

much heat under the circumstances here referred to, and this plan is economical in every way as regards the roots in both cases, which will improve year by year, as each will give more flowers as it gets older. No pots, and therefore no time for potting, will be required, nor half the firing to excite them. If the sashes are taken clean off and put away or used for Cucumber or other frames during the summer, both the classes will mature and the better develop flowering buds than they would if the lights were continued on.

In the beginning of November the old dead leaves should be trimmed off, the surfaces of each cleaned, and some little fine soil sifted over them, about half an inch. At the end of the month commence a small fire, but not too much ; give water if necessary, and air too at first and on all mild days. As soon as the roots begin to show flower, give some weak manure-water. Sheep droppings well diluted may be given a few times before flowering, but never too strong nor too often. If frost appears the frames must be covered at night, but not by day if it can be avoided, and in no case allow the heat to get up too strong at night. After a season or two many hundreds of the Christmas Rose may be cut from such a bed, which will always sell readily at a good price.

### THE COST OF CONSTRUCTING THE PIT.

When a thing of some interest and profit strikes anyone as this idea may do, the next thing is the question, ' What will it cost ? ' And as an answer, the following estimate will be found very near the mark :—

|  | £ | s. | d. |
|---|---|---|---|
| For bricks, mortar, and mason's work, and thirty sashes glazed and painted with three coats complete | 25 | 9 | 6 |
| For boiler: 120 feet three-inch pipe; four elbows India-rubber rings for fitting the pipes; cistern; furnace door and frame; furnace bars; damper and frame, bricks and mortar, and fixing boiler .    . | 9 | 17 | 6 |
| Total    .    . | £35 | 7 | 0 |

I have all the particulars of this estimate by me.

Here, then, is a large and roomy pit at a cheap rate, considering all things, being ten feet wide and sixty feet long, which is equal in capacity and in efficiency to any good-sized forcing house at half the usual cost.

# CHAPTER V.

IT is a well-known and established fact among good floriculturists that it is highly advantageous and effective to devote a whole house, whether it be large or small, to a single class, especially in forcing. There is no doubt some peculiarity belonging to every genus of plants that requires, in a measure, some distinct treatment, under which the class will do much better than when it is treated only partially. The treatment necessary to the proper development of its character can thus be better carried out, and in no case is it more necessary than in the forcing of Roses.

The Rose may be forced with other plants, it is true, but there is no class that requires more individual attention daily than this flower, which when so treated with other plants seldom gets what is absolutely necessary for its proper cultivation, and this from various causes. Light, heat, and moisture are the chief elements required in forcing the Rose. The term 'forcing' may be modified considerably, and some wider range allowed for what is commonly understood by the term by some persons; but in this case it refers to the cultivation of flowers for cutting by February, March, and April.

Some classes of the Rose are much easier to force than others. The Chinas are among these, for they are easy to excite. The Hybrid China, Moss, Gallica, with some exceptions, are more difficult to force well than the former or the Perpetuals and Hybrid Per-

FIG. 2?.—SECTION OF A SIXTY-FEET ROSE-FORCING AND CUCUMBER HOUSE.

Fourteen feet wide, four feet high from ground to eaves, ten feet high to the ridge. To be double-glazed on my plan, without putty.

References to house.—*a*, top ventilators, made to open by rack gearing; B, a set of sliding shutters, two feet by one, along the south side. These work by my cords and pulleys (see figs. 2 and 3).

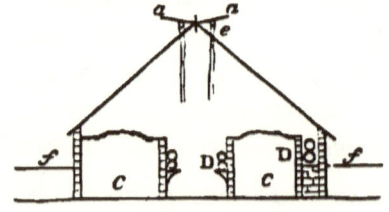

END SECTION OF HOUSE.

References.—*c c*, pit, four feet wide, four feet deep; D D, hot-water pipes; *e*, gearing to open lights, *a*; *f*, ground line.

Cost of this house about 54*l*. 10*s*.

petuals. The object in view must be the chief and fixed rule in this treatment of Roses.

Early Roses may be had by a very simple means, but for commercial purposes some method of doing the thing more to the purpose must be resorted to. I am convinced that there is already an abundance of these commercial forcing houses for all classes of plants as well as for Roses, which might be my excuse for not giving an illustration of what I consider a useful and economical house for the purpose. If the reader refers to most builders' lists of prices for the erection of such a place, he or she will find that my estimate for the same class of house is fully 50 per cent. below theirs. Considering all the advantages connected with the effectual forcing of very early Roses, there can be no better constructed house than one like the Cucumber house. This is capable of holding a great number of large-sized pots. It is sixty feet long, fourteen feet wide, with other good proportions for trade purposes. The pits c c may either be retained or dispensed with, but in my opinion the retention of them, filled with leaves and tan, will be most beneficial in Rose forcing.

Roses will force without bottom heat very well, but they do much better plunged in fermenting materials where a moist temperature can be maintained. It will be found that under such circumstances a more healthy and robust state of the foliage and flower buds will ensue. This house will hold 500 large Roses in nine-inch pots, and capable of giving at the least twenty-five good cut flowers; that would be 12,500 at say 3s. per dozen—1l. 5s. per 100=156l. 5s. for cut Roses from this house from the month of February till the end of April. They may then all be removed from the house and set outside in a sheltered spot and protected from the cold cutting winds by placing mats over them at night for a week or two.

Previous to their removal, cool down the temperature by discontinuing the heat, and by an abundance of air for a week beforehand. Not that Roses are tender, but they may then be used again next year for the same purpose, if not too severely checked by the sudden change of temperature when shifted from the forcing house into the open air. These Roses should be shifted from the pots, or at least turned out and the soil partly shaken out of the roots, and then be re-potted, using a good and entirely fresh compost. This may be done in the month of May, when they may be cut back and well watered, and then plunged in saw-dust, cinder-ashes, or old tan (not fresh tan). Each pot should be set upon a piece of slate to prevent the ingress of worms. The situation for plunging them must be a full sunny one, where they may remain for the summer, when, if kept well supplied with water, with two or three good waterings with liquid manure, a good and vigorous growth will be made for giving flowers the next season. Three or four good strong shoots should be allowed to develop themselves well through the summer, as this is far better than a lot of spray and weak stuff. Cut such out and induce a few strong shoots to make good growth, and when November comes round again they may be lifted from this plung-ing, the pots cleaned off a bit, the drainage looked to, and be taken into the house, but no heat applied at first.

The pruning of these forcing Roses may be done soon after they are placed in the house, but it requires some care, and concerning which I have treated par-ticularly in my 'Fruit Tree and Shrub Pruner.' But for the sake of those who may not care to refer further than to this work for information on this matter, I merely say that those Roses which make long and flexible shoots may be pruned in less closely, and those that make less growth must be cut in closer, such as the old Coupe d'Hébé, Chénedolé, Céline, &c.; which are Hybrid Chinas, strong growers, and are samples of those which must not be pruned in too much; but the Hybrid Perpetuals, Chinas, Tea Chinas, and Gallicas or French Roses, may be cut in much closer.

Now some will perhaps ridicule the idea of my referring to such old Roses as the above, and ask, Why not mention some newer sorts? To this I may fairly answer, Because I am convinced that the old are better. I know that it is one thing to fancy that all new things are best because they are new, but it is quite another thing to prove this and also to find it so by comparison. I am quite convinced that none of the new Roses can excel, if they can equal, the Coupe d'Hébé, Chénedolé, Brennus, William Jesse, the old Crested Provence, &c. All of these are strong and vigorous growers and must not be pruned much, except the last, which may be pruned moderately. But if such as the first four are pruned or cut back too much, no flowers will be obtained. 'Too much!' some will exclaim, 'What is too much?' Well, these Roses must not be cut in closer than from nine inches to one foot six inches within the base of the new wood, and some, such as the Brennus, Chénedolé, &c., must be pruned but little, indeed, merely taking a few inches off the points of the strong shoots will be enough.

It is safer not to prune some Roses at all than to prune them too severely. Maréchal Niel, for instance, although we know it to be a fast-growing climber, will not bear severe pruning, and flowers of this class must never be cut back, but merely thinned out, leaving the wood for flowering at full length. The same thing applies to such as Chénedolé, the Beauty of Billiard, Brennus, &c., besides many of the newer sorts of strong growth.

Pruning must not be deferred long after Roses are placed in a warmer atmosphere. The drainage must be good and free. Plunge the pots quite up to the rims. If they are dry, give water freely. If the heat is not too much, the bottom heat should never exceed 60°. The fermenting material should be put into the pits several weeks before the Roses are introduced into the house, so that the heat may not be in advance, but slightly on the decline. If still at too high a pitch, set the pots on the top of the bed instead of plunging them.

As the Roses begin to show signs of breaking leaf, give them some weak liquid manure. This may consist of one ounce of guano to one gallon of soft tepid water. This will induce a rapid development of the buds and give fine flowers. As the leaf and flower buds appear the aphides may appear also. No time should be lost when these show themselves, but fumigation must be resorted to at once. Syringing every day must also be attended to. This should be done every morning from nine to eleven o'clock. It helps the development of the leaf and bud.

It will not be necessary during the months of December, January, and February to give any air at all to the Roses. They will do well without it under this early forcing; but it will be necessary to admit some at the top of the house after the middle of March to keep down the temperature, which will get too high during clear days. The fire should be lowered and shut off in the morning during very bright and promising sunny days in March, merely just keeping it in, and at three P.M. pull out the damper and stir up the fire, but the heat should not be allowed to rise too high during the night, merely enough to secure progress at a low temperature, say 40° or 45°. The heat of the house during the day may be maintained at 70° or 75°.

In my opinion there is no branch of forcing that will better repay the trouble and expense than a house devoted solely to the production of Moss Roses for the market. All these are especial favourites with the fair sex; and I ask, what can be more beautiful than the half-open bud of a moss rose, with its curious calyx half enveloping the beautiful pink, white, or crimson bud, forming as it were love in a shrine? and of these none deserves more attention than the Crested Provence. This is a rose not generally known; I am convinced, however, that it needs only to be known to be properly appreciated. There is, I think, a mistaken idea about this flower. Some regard it as a moss rose, but I am convinced it is not a true moss, but a Provence, for it bears all the characteristics of that species; on some occasions it will be entirely destitute of moss, and then no one can distinguish it from a true Provence rose. The large foliage and the growth exactly coincide with this kind. Nothing among roses can equal a half-open bud of this class, with its extraordinary and long, mossy-pointed calyx enveloping the lovely pink bud.

To succeed well with this rose, grow it strong, and prune it but very moderately, merely taking a few inches off the points of the last season's growth; or, if the wood made the last season is two feet long, six inches may be cut off the points, and an abundance of flowers will be the result.  Moss roses may, as a rule, be pruned very close.  It is better to select a good many of each sort than to have a great variety for forcing, and I am quite convinced that for cut flowers it is much better to select them from old, well-known prolific sorts, than to have some of the more shy-flowered among the newer kinds.  Many of the delicate Tea roses are very beautiful, but too shy of flower for forcing for the sake of profit.

In packing cut flowers for market, every bud should be wrapped in tissue-paper, slightly twisting the paper carefully round it so as to hold it a little firm, in order to keep it from the air and further development.

# CHAPTER VI.

## THE CAMELLIA HOUSE.

THIS house is on a scale of one-sixteenth of an inch to one foot,[1] so that it is very easy to construct, and will cost but little. It is necessary that a camellia house should run north and south, and thus avoid the strong rays of the sun, as this flower will not bear the full power of the sun. It will lose its colour in the foliage

FIG. 23.—CAMELLIA HOUSE.

Reference to house.—N, north; S, south; a a a a a a a, sliding sashes; B, set of lights hinged on ridge, made to open by cords and rack gearing. The walls to be nine-inch work.

when fully exposed to the sun; for this reason the house in which Camellias are grown should face the west or north-west if only one roof; but for trade purposes, as for cut flowers, I recommend a span roof— one facing east and the other west. Such a house should be glazed with bars not further apart than 12 inches and 1½ thick by 4½ wide, i.e. 1½ + 4½ rafters;

[1] This house is 40 feet long; 22 feet wide: 7 feet high at eaves.

good single clip glazing will answer well (see figs. 7, 8, and 9), omitting the under glazing, although I would even recommend double glazing for them as a safeguard against frost, and more economical as regards firing during the winter. Whenever a house for Camellias alone has to be unavoidably built facing the south with one roof only, *i.e.* a lean-to, it should be made pretty flat and glazed with green glass. In this case the bars may be 18 inches apart. If green glass cannot be had, I advise that a thin transparent green paint be used for a permanency; for I find that plants do much better under green glass during the summer than under clear white glass: especially is this the case with Camellias. When, however, a house for these can be built with a span roof running north and south they will do much better than in a lean-to house.

This house is 14 feet high in the centre, and 7 feet high at the eaves, with 3 feet of glass sashes and 4 feet of brickwork: this gives abundance of head room and elevation enough for large plants all round; 22 feet in width will give plenty of room for a row of pots next the walls all round where one flow and return 4-inch pipe should be placed. A double flow and return pipe will be necessary for a house of this capacity in the northern counties; but one flow and return once round the house will be enough for the western counties. If, however, double glazing is adopted, one flow and return pipe will answer for the colder counties, and none at al will be required in the western counties. The pipes should run round close to the walls of the house; but if a row of plants are planted out into a good peat border next the walls, where they would do well, and nailed on them, they would form a pretty feature, and bear abundantly : then the pipes for heating must be in the pathway in front of the plants. If the middle of the house is permanently planted out, considerable preparation must be made ; which must consist of a deep bed of coarse peat at the bottom, to form a stratum of good soil and drainage. Then, on the top of this, put two feet of maiden loam and pure sandy peat, two parts of the latter to one of the former; these should make up the bed to what is wanted, which should be fully one foot above the original level or the pathway in the house. The bed should be made as firm as possible as the compost is put in, by chopping it to pieces with the spade, mixing turf and soil together and treading it in well, and then it will sink considerably.

The planting of the Camellias should be done as soon as the plants have done flowering, when they should be kept close for a few weeks and a little heat put on to excite them a little, so as to induce some growth, and as soon as a few inches are made, discontinue the fire heat, but keep the house closed till the terminal bud is as large as a white pea, when it should be opened night and day throughout the summer until the end of November, frequently syringing the whole of the plants overhead through the summer to keep them clean. When Camellias are planted in the beds instead of being grown in pots, they naturally grow faster for some years to come, and ultimately become too large for the house, and then it must be made higher : this is both expensive and troublesome. Now there is no real occasion for this extra expense. The Camellia will bear the knife well, but I admit that some small loss is incurred by cutting back too severely, but if the cutting back of overgrown plants is judiciously done, no great loss will be sustained.

The loss referred to is in the flowers for a season, but as the Camellia is such an abundant bearer of flowers (which are frequently three-fourths too numerous on a plant) that they have to be thinned out to get fine specimens, no real loss is sustained by partially cutting back some of the leading branches, if the minor ones are left to flower and fill up. So that by this annual or biennial cutting back of some of the plants they will never get too large for the house; and instead of running up to head, and becoming barren of foliage, and of course of flower, they will maintain a well-clothed appearance down to the ground.

A house of the size of the above, will take forty-eight good strong plants for the middle bed, which may be 15 feet wide, taking four rows of plants at a distance of 3 feet apart each way; the pathways will be 3 feet wide, with a border of 2 feet next the walls, all round the house. The walls will take about forty plants to cover them, ultimately; thus eighty-eight will be required to fill such a house at a moderate calculation. These may consist of any desirable sorts, which will cost in good strong plants, at trade prices, 25*l.* to 30*l.* per 100—well set with flower buds if obtained in the autumn, about October, when they may be planted; or, if deferred till after the flower, and then planted as I have said, which is perhaps the safest, plants of the same size may be had for a lower price. And, if I may be permitted to recommend where to get them both good and cheap, I should say of John Standish & Co., of the Royal Nurseries, Ascot, Berkshire, or of Charles Turner of Slough.

The Camellia, for cut flowers, may be grown in large pots. Pots 15 inches in diameter will do for them for many years; I have grown very fine healthy specimens seven to nine feet high, in 13-inch pots, for seven years successively, by giving them some liquid manure once a week, containing half-an-ounce of guano to one gallon of water,—not more must be given. The advantages of growing the Camellia in pots or tubs are that they can be removed from the house, after the flower buds are formed, to a sheltered spot on the north side of a high wall or hedge, where little or no sun can come to them during the summer. I have found this an excellent method for this flower, especially when they are obliged to be grown in a clear glass south-house; under such circumstances the poor Camellias suffer much. The foliage loses its natural, deep glossy green, and the flower buds open prematurely.

There is but one time in the whole season when the Camellia will bear a forcing temperature, and that is immediately after it has flowered, till the buds are formed, as I have previously said. All that is required for it at other times is merely to ward off protracted frosts. For the propagation of it, I beg to refer the reader to my 'Tree Planter and Plant Propagator.'

As a commercial affair, I know of few things that will better repay the trouble and outlay than a house of permanent Camellias for cut flowers. We will suppose, for instance, that such a house will take close upon one hundred plants to stock it, and that these will each average ten flowers the first season after planting, at only 10s. per dozen. That would give more than 40l. worth the first year; and without any other expense except a little fuel and time. Each plant will progress in productiveness year by year, for, say, as long as a man is likely to live, beginning when he is a young

man.   Some may say, it is a fine calculation as regards
figures.   So it is, I admit; but when I calculate, I do
so from my own knowledge and judgment.

The cost of constructing the camellia house may be
estimated as below :—

|  | £ | s. | d. |
|---|---|---|---|
| Eighty-four rafters, thirteen feet long, four and a half inches by one and a half . . . . | | | |
| Two hundred and four feet sill and eaves plate | | | |
| Forty feet ridge board, four and a half inches by one and a half . . . . . . . | | | |
| One hundred and forty-six feet run, one and a half inches by one and a half, for sashes, and making them . . . . . . . | | | |
| One hundred and forty-one feet run, one and a half inch by one and a half, for fixed sash bars in sides . . . . . . . . | | | |
| Fifty-six feet run, one and a half inches by one and a half, for fixed sash, for gable end . . | | | |
| Stuff, and making fourteen sash ventilators at top . . . . . . . . . | | | |
| One good door, and making . , . . . | | | |
| One thousand three hundred and sixty feet twenty-one-ounce glass, twenty inches by twelve, and carriage . . . . . . | | | |
| Seven hundred and thirty-six clips for glazing . | | | |
| All the glazing . . . . . . . | | | |
| Six thousand three hundred and sixty bricks and carriage . . . . . . . | | | |
| Masons' work, and mortar . . . . . | 43 | 3 | 6 |
| Heating apparatus and fixing . . . . | 30 | 0 | 0 |
| | £73 | 3 | 6 |

By comparison this estimate, although of the best
materials and workmanship, is considerably less than
50 per cent. of the usual prices for building such a
house.   Many will have some doubt about the workmanship, and ask how it can be done ?   But I am fully
prepared to show how it is to be done.

# CHAPTER VII.

THE Ferns are amongst our most favoured foliaged plants, and well deserve to be such esteemed favourites, for they are not like other classes of plants, most of which have a season of display, and then relapse into a state of comparative disinterest; but the family of ferns as a tribe maintain an interest which never flags : this arises from their beautiful form and evergreen character. Let a class of plants be what it may as regards beauty while in foliage and flower, the day that it ceases flowering and loses its foliage it is looked upon (by an amateur at least) as a thing of the past; but it is never so with the family of Ferns.

Since, then, ferns are so eagerly sought after, and appreciated by everybody, I am at a loss to discover a sufficient reason why we find so few glass-houses devoted entirely to the culture of this tribe, for there is no class of plants so easy to grow; although I know some persons do not succeed very well with them. In the first place glass-houses for growing them frequently are not situated where they should be; and secondly, they are not glazed with proper glass for the situation the house occupies. I recommend that at all times a house, entirely devoted to the growing of ferns, should be constructed so as to face the north or west, or north-east, but never to face full south. Let amateurs and young gardeners take a walk along some lane or by-road where Ferns grow naturally, and they will no doubt see them on both sides of the lane, growing on the banks; one side may be facing the sun all day, the other will be facing the north, where no sun can come to them. Now just observe the difference of colour in the same species! Those growing where the sun plays upon them are stunted and brown; the others on the opposite side are so far different in character and colour that one is ready to conclude that the same varieties are two different species. Now this should be a lesson in the culture of all Ferns, whether hardy or not. I have always found that when Ferns under glass are much exposed to a strong light, they are of a less deep green in colour than when shaded.

The Fern tribe may be partly compared to the Heath family in the matter of water. If a Heath gets thoroughly dry through the ball, nothing can save that plant from death; but it is not quite the same with the Fern, for if one of the latter gets thoroughly dry a few times, it is ten to one if it lives; certainly the present Fronds will die off, and perhaps the root too. Ferns luxuriate in a brisk moist heat; but they may be grown without much heat—I mean the greenhouse sorts—but it is necessary to be provided with some means of heating the house, to ward off frosts.

When a fernery is to be built, if it must be facing the south, which sometimes cannot be avoided in the case of amateurs, the top of the house should be double glazed, the top or outside layer of glass being of a pale green colour, and the under layer being of white glass. I recommend double glazing, because then, amateurs can grow Ferns well, without much fire-heat, or none at all during the summer. It looks expensive to double glaze, but I am prepared to show that, on my plan of ' double glazing,' it is no more so than single glazing as a rule.

A fernery needs very little or no ventilation, except when it is built facing the sun : then some top ventilation is necessary for the summer, but none from September till April. If the roof is double glazed with clips on the fixed vertical bar, and with green glass or the top painted with semi-transparent paint laid on with a large brush, very little trouble will arise in growing Ferns successfully. They will, under these circumstances, maintain a very even character, being attended by a constant and equal temperature, which is the very thing for them. During the winter months a few cinders or a little coke should be put into a proper stove to keep up a healthy temperature, when the most delicate classes may be grown successfully. If the fernery has to be built facing the south, be careful not to have the angle of the roof of too sharp a pitch : an angle of 30° is quite enough for such an aspect, but for a northern or north-western one, an angle of 32° may be adopted, as no sun can then get at the plants to affect them. If the fernery is facing the north, it may be double glazed with Belgium green glass or with common white, but it will be found that they will do much better under green glass than under white.

It is necessary for trade purposes to stimulate ferns as much as possible to keep up successional fronds for cutting or for plants to supply customers. To do this, different departments connected with Fern culture are required ; one not too hot, for large specimens from which fronds may be cut; one for their propagation by seed and by division ; and another for bringing on the specimens or the young plants for sale. The house for seedlings &c. (which should be partially under ground) must always be kept close with a good moist heat ; that for bringing them on for specimens and for sale should be kept close with a moderate heat ; and the one for the well-developed specimens may be kept moderately moist with ventilation at the top of the house, but none at the sides. By this arrangement the plants will be so far hardened that neither the cut fronds for bouquets, nor the plants for decoration or sale, will suffer so much as they often do from the fact of their being taken straight from a high temperature and exposed to a very low one. The invariable consequence is either death, or what is as bad, a loss of all the points of future beauty.

The soil most suitable for Ferns is, no doubt, one composed of two parts fine sandy peat and one part good tender maiden loam, the latter not made too fine, but chopped up with the spade turf and all and well mixed with the peat. The drainage for large pots must be well secured by first placing some good-sized crocks over the bottoms of them, and on these a good layer of smaller shreds, and then some siftings of the peat. The old fronds should be cut out to make room for the new ones, and an abundance of soft and tepid water must be given to all Ferns when growing, and that is always when they are in a moist heat, especially the maiden-hair class. There are, however, a few exceptions to this rule. There is what is called the Elkshorn, or Alcicorne, or *Platycerium Alcicorne* ; some call it Stagshorn : it belongs to the *Polypodiums*. This Fern

is certainly a curiosity: it neither requires soil nor
water to grow in, but merely to be fastened upon a block
of rustic wood, or it may be placed in a basket or
seed-pan or pot. If grown in the first-named way, it
should have a little moss and be tacked on to the
block, or the pan or pot may be filled up tight with
moss, and the plant tied on, and then suspended by
a wire from the roof of the fernery or green-house,
where it will grow for many years without any further
trouble. This plant rather differs from the Polypody
vulgare which we find growing so plentifully upon
wood along the road sides, and which seems to draw
its nourishment from the branch to which it adheres,
while the Alcicorne lives upon its own natural resources.
The Wall Rue or *Asplenium Ruta-Muraria* and
Ceterach, which grow upon dry walls, are of this self-
sustaining class, but there are none that seem capable
of this so much as the first-named.

To be successful in propagating Ferns, the house
should be close, low and warm, having the walls
lined with turfy peat-sods, the under side of which
should be placed outermost and kept up either by long
hook nails, or wall hooks, or by bars of wood fastened
with hooks to the wall. Some moss may be stuffed
between the joints of the sods, which will retain
moisture and serve as receptacles for seed, which may
be sown all over these sod-lined walls. The seed should
be first well soaked with water by syringing, and then
sown all over the walls and never disturbed afterwards.
Neither should they be heavily syringed, for this would
wash the seed off. Peat sods may also be placed under
the seeding fronds which will catch the seed as it falls.

To be successful in raising new sorts, gather the

seed of the different species and put it into a fine paper packet, sealed quite close, and put this packet into your waistcoat pocket and carry it there for a month. Then sow it in seed pans filled with rough peat, well watered before sowing ; and after it is sown place a bell glass over it and keep the pans in a shady place in the warm house. Fern seed soon germinates.

The most desirable sorts are the Adiantums, which genus includes the Maiden-hairs :—the Farleyense, A. cuneatum, Formosum, Concinnum, Gracillinum, a most delicate Fern, and Trapeziforme, a splendid foliaged kind. Onoclea sensibilis, another very handsome light green and fine bold foliaged sort; Petris serrulata, and P. crestata, Gymnogramma chrysophilla, the Golden Fern, and the Parsley Fern are all very beautiful and handsome varieties.

# CHAPTER VIII.

## THE PINK AND CARNATION FORCING HOUSE.

FROM a commercial point of view these flowers are not much understood as a lucrative class for forcing.

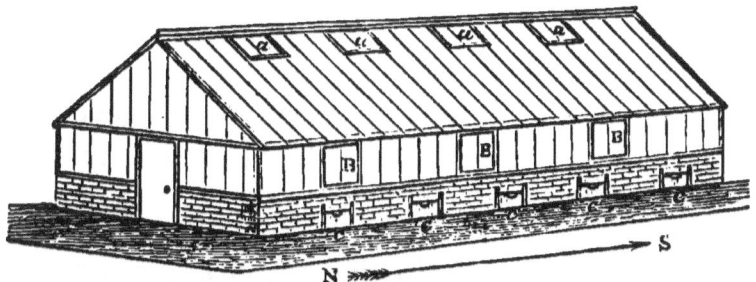

FIG. 24.—SECTION OF A SIXTY-FEET SPAN-ROOF CARNATION HOUSE, EIGHTEEN FEET WIDE.

Reference to plan.—*a a a a*, top ventilators ; B B B, sliding sashes ; *c c c c c*, zinc shutters, made to lift up and down in runs for the admission of air, when the sashes, 'B,' cannot be opened ; DD, staging all round the house, two feet three inches wide, to hold three rows of carnations ; E, the centre stand, showing how the fixed troughs are made for the plants, nine inches wide and seven inches deep ; F, hot-water pipes ; G, pathway.

END SECTION OF HOUSE.

Nor do many seem to succeed well with them. I attribute failure chiefly to one cause : like most other

plants that are intended for forcing, they must be prepared for some time previously, and perhaps upon the
whole, Pinks and Carnations require more of this
preliminary preparation than any other class.  A failure
can scarcely arise if proper steps are taken to fit the
plants to the work, nor is there anything that will better
repay the trouble; for a strong and well developed
Pink or Carnation will give an abundance of fine flowers
which may fetch from 2s. to 4s. per dozen, in the
months of March and April.

Now I will suppose a house capable of holding 2,000
plants, and that each of these will give, say only 10
good flowers; this, however, is a low calculation, nume-
rically speaking; but to make sure, we will say 10 good
flowers to each plant, these at 3d. each (the lowest
price): 20,000 flowers at 1l. 5s. per 100 = 125l. per
10,000; double this sum and we have the net sum of
250l. for Pink and Carnation flowers from this house.
Now some will say, ' It is easy to calculate, but can you
do it ?'  Well, I will see presently, but I beg to remind
the reader that this, like making 620l. from one acre
of land, is not to be done by putting down figures, nor
by talking about it, and glorying over the results by
anticipation, nor without some trouble, good judgment
and expense too.   Those who dream of getting 20,000
flowers, and 250l. cash, must not deviate one step from
the royal road to such success ; and I would advise no
one to calculate upon such results, except they first
count the cost, or rather make up their mind whether
they can or will do as I should do; men frequently
reckon upon great results without lawfully striving to
obtain them; others censure an idea which is to all
intents and purposes quite practicable, and condemn

the idea with a 'pooh,' simply because they have never tried it, or never allowed their minds to think about it. The first thing to do is to get a stock of suitable Pinks and Carnations, and the next thing is to know how and when to propagate them. This is simple enough if those who undertake the matter do but begin at the proper place and persevere to the end. I will suppose that a man wishes to produce 2,000 Pink and Carnation plants for forcing, and such as will not disappoint him in the results. How many stock plants must he get at once to do this in one season? and when must he get them? are the most important questions. If he wishes to possess 1,000 plants fit for forcing of each class, he must buy them in the month of September: 50 or 60 well-established, early-struck Pinks of the sorts recommended, and 150 old but good plants of the Carnation. The last season pipings, or layers, may be used, but unless the last of these are very strong, they will not do. These must be two-year-old plants in pots and of a good stocky character, for the Carnation will not yield so many pipings as the Pink per plant, at the same age. The 50 or 60 Pinks, if good and early-struck stuff, will do; but the Carnations will not, unless they are healthy and stocky.

Now we may suppose that we have the plants at nome, and in good pots, all growing. Place them in a mild heat, in a pit or house; continue to encourage them to grow, and as soon as a batch of good pipings can be had, take them off with three or four joints, and prepare each in the usual manner; then, having a lot of deep seed-pans ready—square ones are the best for economising the room, but the former are necessary to get depth enough—previous to preparing the pipings, fill a dozen or two of the pans with a compost of one part maiden loam sifted fine through a quarter or three-eighths of an inch mesh sieve, two parts fine-sifted leaf-mould, and one part silver sand, well mixed together. First, place a few crocks over the holes in the bottom of the pans, then a little of the siftings over them, and finally fill up to the rims, making it quite firm; then prepare the pipings in the usual way by cutting the base of the third or fourth joint at right angles im-mediately below the joint, but not into it, so as to leave one-sixteenth of an inch below it. Cut with a razor-edged small knife—a penknife will do very well. As soon as enough are made to fill one pan, insert the pipings with a small pointed stick not larger than a lead pencil, at one inch apart all over the pans; and give a thorough soaking with water through a fine rose. Then place the pans, as they are filled, on a mild bottom heat, over a tank or heated pit, and keep the house or pit close till the pipings are struck, which will be with-in three weeks with the Pinks, and a month with the Carnations.

As soon as they are well struck give them air, or place the pans containing the plants in a cooler house or pit, to harden off a little, say for a week. Then prick them off into other pans or boxes, about two inches apart, water, and return them to the house or a warm pit with a good light. As the plants get strength and begin to grow, nip out the central point; this will in-duce a bushy growth. It will now be about the end of March or beginning of April: so admit an abundance of air daily, and by the beginning of May the plants will all be in good order for planting out. Now choose a nice mellow spot of ground in an open sunny place;

manure it well, and dig it, breaking it fine, and mix
the manure thoroughly with the soil; and just here I
would say that there is no manure which suits Pinks
and Carnations so well as horse droppings from the
roads, swept up with some sand. Put the manure on
pretty thick: six barrowfuls to one perch, or about thirty
square yards, is not too much. It will take about six
square perches of ground to hold 2,000 plants, including the paths, &c., at ten inches apart. The ground
should be manured and dug in the month of March,
then it will get well pulverised, and when a nice shower
of rain comes about the end of April, it will be in first-
class order for the young plants. Strike the ground
out into four-feet beds, work over the surface with a
hoe, and then rake it over with a coarse rake, and put
out the plants with a trowel, letting them down into
the soil quite up to the leaves; and when a bed is
planted, give it a good soaking with water to settle the
soil well to the plants.

As the plants advance in growth, nip out every young
shoot to induce a bushy habit; and when September
comes they will be, or should be, large and fine plants,
of the size of a cheese plate, compact and full of young
stuff that will give flowering stems; but none of these
must be allowed to remain on the plants that spring up
from them while in the beds; if any do come, nip them
off at once as soon as they appear.

About the end of September the plants may be
carefully lifted with a large trowel, having a good ball
of earth to each plant. To make sure of doing this
properly, before taking them up give each bed a heavy
soaking with water the previous evening. As each one
is lifted, place it in a plant-barrow direct, and when it

is full, carry them to the house where they are to flower, and place them in their flowering quarters. Now comes the most economical method of doing this. Some persons force them in pots, but they never do so well as when bedded in boxes made on purpose ; besides they are more troublesome to pot than to bed, and do not take so much room as when grown in pots. These boxes may be permanent, for they may be made out of the stage or stand—that is, the staging in the house may be made into troughs instead of open work, each step or shelf being a long box or trough, nine inches wide and seven inches deep; or separate and portable boxes, of the same width and depth, may be used. Place each plant, as you take it from the barrow, in its place at once, without changing and shifting, as the less they are moved about, the less danger there is of losing the soil from the balls. The plants may be placed as close as they can be, or nearly so, filling up the spaces around each, as you proceed, with fine soil like that used for striking the pipings, and fitting it in firmly, filling up also to the top of each trough or box. When all are in, give them a good watering ; shade the house for a short time at first, till the plants get established, frequently syringing them overhead. Some air must be admitted to dry them off, or some of the foliage of the Pinks, being thick, will probably rot off. Keep up a heat of 55° or 60°, admitting air during October, and on the mild days in November. When air cannot be given them by opening the front lights, draw up the zinc shutters c, which will admit it without lowering the temperature, as the air will, in this way, come into immediate contact with the hot-water pipes. Keep up the temperature, give plenty of water, and once a week some liquid manure ; and you will not be disappointed as regards the results.

The ordinary way and time for striking pipings, or making layers, of the Carnation and Pink will not do for forcing plants the same season, as two years are required to make plants like those I now describe ; and then such plants must not be allowed to flower, for they will not be such good ones as those struck and pushed on as these are.

There are many sorts of Pinks and Carnations that may be used for forcing, but the following seem to be the best of the Pinks—the old Anne Boleyn, Coccinea, Lady Blanche, Lord Lyons, Paddington, Mrs. Pettifeer, and a variety besides ; and of the Carnations—Miss Jolliffe, La Zouave, Covent Garden Scarlet, Valiant, White Nun, Rosy Morn, Mercury, &c. Almost any free-flowering Pink and Carnation may be forced ; but those that are shy of flower, and that grow long and thin in the grass, are not fit for this purpose ; but any of the kind that opens freely, and without bursting the pod, may be used for forcing. Mr. Charles Turner of Slough is the most likely man to get a good selection from, for this purpose. Get the stocks as early as they can be had, which I think I have said is in September.

The house I recommend is the sixty feet span ; eighteen feet wide, twelve feet high at the ridge, and five feet high in front, as the illustration shows, heated with four-inch pipe, and one of those inexpensive saddle boilers before referred to. The whole cost of such a house may be estimated at 42l. 18s., as follows (without the heating and the staging, for which 35l. more must be added) :—

Eighty-two rafters, twelve feet long, four and a half inches by one and a half.

Sixty feet ridge board, four and a half inches by one and a half.

Two hundred and forty feet eaves and sill plate, two inches by four and a half.

Four hundred and twenty-four feet sash bars, for ends and fronts.

One good door, lock, and key.

Two thousand feet twenty-one-ounce glass, eighteen inches by twelve, and carriage for two hundred miles.

Eight hundred and eighty glazing clips, and glazing.

One thousand seven hundred and nineteen stock bricks, at 1*l.* 10*s.* per thousand, and carriage for five miles.

Masons' work, mortar, &c.

Painting and paint.

Fourteen zinc shutters and frames.

Six set of gearing for top ventilators, in all £42 18*s.*

Add 25*l.* for a boiler and connections, and 10*l.* for staging.

Total, for house sixty feet long by eighteen feet wide, five feet high in front, twelve feet high to ridge, £77 18*s.*

All the materials and work to be good : this is less than half the usual cost for such a house.

Now if such a place were built and ready by August, and the stock of Pinks and Carnations purchased by the end of September, and put to work, the profits arising from the sale of the flowers would pay for the building of the house, and then leave a handsome surplus for the trouble. The cost of the stock depends upon the kind and strength of the plants; but good sorts and good plants can be had in Pinks at 18*s.* per dozen, and in Carnations at 2*l.* per dozen ; less by the hundred, and in the trade ; but it is useless to think about obtaining a number of plants, fit for forcing, and capable of giving the requisite quantity of flowers, unless these steps are taken.

The house illustrated above will hold 2,000 plants,

as I have said, bedding them into the troughs made as fixtures, which, if constructed of good three-quarter-inch yellow deal, will last for many years; so that there will be no expense as regards pots.

# CHAPTER IX.

THE cultivation of Fancy Pelargoniums is so well known and appreciated, that but few remarks are necessary to bring it into favour, or to induce most people to commence growing them for the purpose of sale. But as there may be some who never tried what can be done by cultivating this popular flower, I may be excused for making a few observations about it.

There are many classes of this tribe, but none scarcely comparable to the large-flowered fancy sorts. These are most attractive when well grown, and are always saleable at good prices ; of late years the Zonal and Nosegay classes have come into much repute, on account of their being all but perpetual flowerers, being also less difficult to grow than some of the fancy show sorts. The Tricolors are certainly beautiful in the foliage, and that is all ; but they are in most cases difficult to grow well, requiring a good and even temperature of a moderately high degree, with good soil and pot room. They are, however, useful for cut foliage to place outside a bouquet, and for a button-hole ; but there is no class more favoured than the original type of the Fancy Pelargonium, such as Queen Victoria, Favourite, Acme, Fanny Gair, &c.

But it is not now my purpose to make lists of any

plants, for catalogues furnish these in abundance, many of them being descriptive as well : the most suitable house and how to fill it, is the subject which I am writing about. The span-roof is no doubt the best form of house that can be used for the proper culture of Pelargoniums, the same kind and of the same construction as I recommend for the Carnation. This may be used with equal advantage, except that no troughs for the stand are required, as these flowers must be grown in pots. All good growers recommend the span-roof for Geranium growing; but if this has one full south roof, the other can get no direct rays from the sun, and the plants on the north stage will be drawn, and later than those on the south side ; so to remedy this evil I re- commend that the house be set north and south, as for the Pink and Carnation house ; then each roof will get a portion of the sunshine. The house may not be quite of so early a kind, but if it is glazed eighteen or twenty inches apart from rafter to rafter, there will be an abundance of good light, and indirect rays from the sun sufficient to grow the Geranium early and well ; and, by-the-bye, a house so situated will be much better for a protracted flowering than one facing the south, nor will so much shading of the plants, when they are in flower, be required as when one side is full south.

The angle of this roof is such as to throw plenty of good light among the plants, which is a most important element for the growing of good dwarf, healthy, and handsome specimens. The old houses in which Pelargoniums used to be grown (and are now sometimes) are just the sort to produce the drawn-up plants which we see from such constructions—plants with stems a foot or eighteen inches high to the flower, and in, per-

haps, a five-inch pot.   But now that our eyes are opened
to the various requirements of plants, we devise better
means for growing them, so as not only to produce more
handsome specimens, but also of a dwarfer character,
which displays their colours to greater advantage.

A forcing house of the dimensions and construction
of the one for the Pink and Carnation is sufficiently
capacious for a man to get a living from, with the addition of a few pits or frames; and I will now show how
it is to be done.   This house will hold, first, 1060 well-
grown Geraniums, in five-inch pots; to be succeeded
by 860 Balsams, in eight-inch pots, for sale as plants,
or for seed; or 800 Begonias, or 1,200 Fuchsias, or
1,200 various plants; all of which may be valued at
1s. each, besides the Geraniums, which may be put at
the same figure at the least.

The Balsams may be estimated at 2s. 6d. per pot,
whether grown for seed or sold as plants.   In each case
the Geraniums will be gone from the house before the
succeeding batch of plants will require the room.   The
Geraniums will have to be nursed and housed in the
same place all the winter, and flowered there; but the
Balsams need not be raised before April, and can then
be reared in a good frame or pit, and be potted off into
small pots, in readiness for shifting into the eight-inch
ones as soon as the Geraniums are gone.

I have always found Messrs. Waite, Burnell, & Co.
supply good reliable articles, and if at any time anything
did not prove so good as might be expected, they were
always ready and willing to throw something off the
cost.   I have dealt with them for many years, and can
vouch for what I say.   This firm seems to me to be the

trade resort for the profession generally; and next comes Sutton—first or last, they bear a good name.

The Geraniums should be propagated annually from cuttings of the short-jointed young stuff taken off with a small heel of the solid young wood, as early as it can be had, for very early and strong young plants, to flower in May or the beginning of June. As soon as the cuttings are well rooted, pot them off into small pots singly— large 60-size pots—three and a half inches in diametei ; and nip out the point of every plant, and continue to do so, as soon as young growth is made of two inches in length, until the middle of March, when the stopping should be discontinued, or else the flowering will be late. The longer the stopping is continued, the later will be the flower. The main thing is to strike the plants as early as possible, say about May or the beginning of June, and then get the young plants on well, and stop them so as to form them dwarf and quite stemless, covering a five-and-a-half-inch pot before the winter ; then the foundation for a fine flower, and an early one too, is laid.

In the month of October (earlier if a wet season) place the plants in the house where they are to remain for the winter, admitting all the air possible to them. Give no fire heat at first, except the weather is very wet and cold, then a little may be put on to drive off the damp, admitting an abundance of air daily, to keep the plants dry about the foliage, and not too moist about the root. The chief thing is not to excite the plants any more than is necessary at this time, nor indeed till the month of March, when more stimulants may be given them; not, however, in the shape of heat, but in that of very weak liquid manure once a week from March until they are in flower. But I particularly advise that no *guano*, or any strong stimulant, be given them at any time, for I have found that when overdoses of guano have been administered, to force plants into large specimens, much mischief has been done in the way of ' spot,' &c.   It is far better to err on the safe side, and not to give enough, than to give the plants very strong doses of liquid manure.   The best time to do this, no doubt, is when they are showing flower, *i.e.* when the flower-buds are formed.

Geraniums especially require to be kept as quiet as possible during the dull months of winter ; all, or nearly all, the growth to form a good symmetrical plant should be made before November.   Then the main thing is to keep the plants half dry and quiet through the next three or four dull months.

Now, by a moderate calculation, this house, which is sixty feet long, and will not cost more than 80*l.* including everything, will return a profit of 156*l.*, 130*l.*, or 110*l.*, according to what is to follow the Geraniums. Of course there is a deduction to be made for pots, soil, and a little firing ; the fuel may be put at 25*s.* per month, 10*l.* for pots, with 1*l.* for soil for potting, more or less, according to distance: total expenses, say, 17*l.* 6*s.* besides time—which is a profit worth trying for.

Generally the aphides will trouble the Geraniums as soon as the warm weather comes, and they are often very troublesome in the spring.   No time must be lost when they appear, but the fumigation must be done at once.   Do not syringe the plants overhead, for this will cause defect in the foliage, spot, &c.   No more shading should be given to a Pelargonium house than can be avoided, for this draws the plants and occasions a bad colour in the leaf.   If the house is set with its end to the south, with the door there, then a very slight shading, while they are in flower, will be required ; but none at all for a trade house, as it is the best policy in business to despatch the whole of what is ready at once. Get the house clear, and fill it with a second batch of whatever is most saleable.

# CHAPTER X.

IN order to be successful in growing Gesneraceous plants, either the house for them must be facing the east or west, or else it must be shaded. The kind of house similar to that recommended for the Geranium, and set the same way, is as good as anything for this class of plants, except that the roof should be double-glazed, and the rafters placed much closer together, as they require no strong sunlight; on the contrary, this must be avoided. If a southern aspect is adopted, some permanent evergreen shade must be employed for the south roof, otherwise this class will get injured by the strong rays of the sun in their beautiful foliage, on account of which they are considered so handsome.

The foliage of some of these species is handsomely marked, while others are of a deep velvety green; and in either case, if exposed to the strong rays of the sun, they get scorched and then lose the beauty for which they are so much admired. This class includes the lovely free-flowering Achimenes with its multitudinous varieties; the glorious and unique family of Gloxinias, which must be seen to form an adequate idea of their beauty when in foliage as well as in flower; the Plectopoma, a sort of half Achimenes and half Gloxinia; the Gesnera Zebrina and its varieties; the Streptocarpus, with its curious construction; the Nigella, a kind of Gesnera with very handsome foliage and exquisite flowers, which are produced in winter, making them valuable for cut flowers: these all require a good house, and in general a brisk and lively heat—a stove heat of 70° to 80° is required to grow them well. The house for all these should be double-glazed.

The Achimenes and Streptocarpus may be grown in a common greenhouse through the summer, but must first be started into growth in a good heat; but in the colder counties it is necessary to grow all of them in a temperature of 70° up to 80° with shade. In my opinion, a house filled with Gesneras of all classes possesses a feature and a charm quite uncommon for those who delight in what is really gorgeous and handsome, combined with what may be called exquisite. If we refer only to the tribe of the Gloxinia, this is fully realised; but add to this the other species and their varieties, and then we find that these words fall into insignificance as descriptive of what is meant by the terms 'handsome, beautiful, and exquisite;' for no words can convey any adequate idea of what they really are when well grown and in masses.

None of these are difficult to grow: the chief thing is to preserve the roots well through the winter or the time when they are dormant, and to have a good compost of half-dry leaf-mould, peat, maiden loam, and silver sand to start them in, when they are to be excited, and a brisk heat to continue them in whenever that is done, and to maintain a good even temperature while they are growing, never allowing the full power of the sun to fall upon them.

The house recommended for the Geraniums may be

used for these with double the amount of hot-water pipes, and a boiler capable of heating them, to be double-glazed, with clips on my plan, according to fig. 7 or 9. The double glazing of this house is essential for these plants, as they are, many of them, winter flowerers, and it is the best for such a class of tender plants, being safe, certain, and economical. If the house containing this class of plants does, or must, face the south, then select some appropriate climber for the south roof, and I know of none better suited for this purpose than an Allamanda, or a Jasminum, or a Bougainvillea glabra; each of these may be trained as you please, covering the roof with a certain number of permanent leaders and then spurred in as for a vine. Thus the climber may be made to cover the roof thickly, or to form a half-shade, which is the proper thing for Gesneraceous plants : too much shade is not good for them, but only so much as will break the full power of the light.

In attempting to grow this class of plants, it is necessary to be careful and not to give the roots any water when they are first excited, but to allow them to make some little growth and then to give water sufficient to half-wet the soil all through. The drainage must be perfect, that is, one that will not admit of the settlement of any water, but allow it to pass off directly; thus the danger of too much water will be obviated.

The tribe of Gloxinias are perhaps among our best Gesneraceous plants. They may be raised from seed, but as so few of them raised in this way are of much commercial value, it is quite a speculation to do so. It is much better to purchase a dozen or two well-known sorts and to propagate them by cuttings of the leaves and save the seed yourself. Then perhaps there is a better chance of getting more good seedlings from such seed than there is from the seed generally sold. After the plants have spent themselves in flowering allow the bulbs to dry off gradually till they are quite dry; then keep them so till the early spring, when they may be subjected to a brisk heat, and when signs of growth appear, give them some water carefully, and as soon as an inch of growth is made (if they are in the pots in which they flowered last season), shake them out and the old soil from the roots also, and re-pot them. In the case of the real Gesneras the same treatment recommended for the Achimenes may be adopted; that is, dry them off thoroughly after flowering, leaving them in the pots, and keeping the bulbs in a dry and warm place such as the back shelves of a plant-stove where no drip can fall upon the roots. This may be done either in the early or late spring, for these may be started at all seasons from December till May according to the time when they are required to flower.

In the case of the Gesneras, Achimenes, Plectopomas, &c., the dry roots may be shaken out of the soil, moss, &c. in which they have flowered the last season and in which they have been kept during the months of dormancy. The roots should then be planted in fine sifted half-dry leaf-mould one part, maiden loam one part, good peat one part, and silver sand one part, well mixed together. Place the roots thickly in this soil in deep seed-pans and cover them with from one and a half to two inches of the same light soil; one inch will do for the Achimenes. Set the pans on bottom heat, give no water till they have made an inch of growth,

K

then give tepid water so as to wet the soil fairly through, and shade them (especially the Gesneras and Achimenes) from the sun; for if the sun's rays fall upon the foliage it will be discoloured and the plants spoilt as regards their beauty for the season. As soon as these have made say two inches of young growth, pot them off into five-inch pots, placing three roots in each pot. The Gesnera zebrina and this class should have a six-inch pot for three roots, using a little stronger compost, *i.e.* one having more loam in it.

The Plectopomas and Achimenes may be made into exquisite ornaments for the conservatory by bedding them in moss and fine sifted leaf-mould, and filling globular wire baskets with handles, by which they may be suspended by means of a wire from the roof of a lofty house. This is especially the case with the free-flowering and clear-coloured Achimenes, such as old longiflora (blue) and longiflora alba, two remarkable and showy sorts; these will appear almost of celestial beauty for many weeks. To meet the object in view perfectly, each basket must be well filled or there will be a defect in the display. The plants should be bedded in with the moss in layers with their points showing out all round, but not more than three inches apart. A single basket of the ordinary size will take perhaps fifty, sixty, or eighty plants; but as the Achimenes are multiplied so fast and so easily, it does not take much to fill a dozen or two of such baskets.

It is quite astonishing what a number of fine bulbs one of these baskets will turn out in one season. The moss and leaf-mould together seem exactly the thing for them; the rhizomes run into it, forming bulbs in abundance which I find are larger and much healthier than when grown merely in the soil. If they are potted off for flowering, a good handful of moss should be placed in the bottom of each pot. Weak stimulants may be given to all the Gesneras during the flowering. It will be necessary to provide a double set of hot-water pipes for this house.

# CHAPTER XI.

THE Calceolaria and Cineraria are two such well-known species that they need no description, although for

FIG. 25.—SECTION OF A SIXTY-FEET SPAN-ROOF CARNATION HOUSE, EIGHTEEN FEET WIDE.

Reference to plan.—*a a a a*, top ventilators; B B B, sliding sashes; *c c c c c*, zinc shutters, made to lift up and down in runs for the admission of air, when the sashes, 'B,' cannot be opened; D D, staging all round the house, two feet three inches wide, to hold three rows of carnations; E, the centre stand, showing how the fixed troughs are made for the plants, nine inches wide and seven inches deep; F, hot-water pipes; G, pathway.

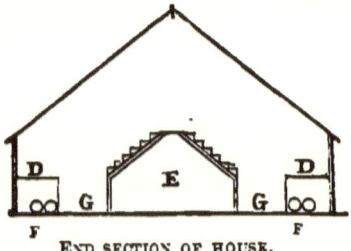

END SECTION OF HOUSE.

all that, practical treatises never seem to be out of place regarding them. They are usually considered

difficult plants to grow well—at least this is the com-
plaint of amateurs. ' Ah! ' they say—' we like them, but
they are so much infested with or liable to the insect ; '
so they give up the idea of growing them.

I know very well that to grow either of them in a
mixed collection of plants is far more difficult than it is
to grow them in a house by themselves. This is why I
particularly wish to impress upon the reader the necessity of devoting a house almost entirely, if not quite, to
the exclusive growing of these and some other plants,
as complete collections of the same species and their
varieties. The difference required in the treatment of
the various genera call aloud for the exclusive devotion
of compartments of houses, or departments devoted solely
to each and its allies. No one can grow Geraniums and
Calceolarias and Cinerarias all together at one and the
same time ; by attempting to do so a miserable failure
is the result, and extorts complaints against these individual species. Glass is now cheap, and by following
up my method in the construction of houses, and by the
economical way of glazing, heating, &c. much larger
houses can be built for the same prices usually paid for
places half the size. I can guarantee this, and I am
fully prepared to give full illustrations and detailed
estimates with practical information how to do it.

The house illustrated above, which is precisely the
same as for the forcing of the Pink and Carnation, costs
about half the amount that most professional builders
charge for the construction of a similar place. I see by
the price lists of various builders I have now by me that
such a house complete will cost not less than 155*l.*,
whereas my estimate is 77*l.* 18*s.* complete, without the
stage for the plants. Then why not devote a house to

the prize-growing of these two beautiful subjects? What will grow the Cineraria will also grow the Calceolaria, *i.e.* the same house will do for both in succession.

I want to show again how effective and interesting such a house may be made with only these two classes. It is considerably more difficult to grow a lot of miscellaneous plants in one house, than one or two species in the same. Many no doubt have been struck with the idea of realising ' 176*l*. from three glass houses,' as I have said may be done in a business way, in my 'Multum-in-parvo Gardening;' but I must say again, that if it can be done in a business way, then it is surely worth while to try the same thing in the way of pleasure for the sake of the amount of variety in the aggregate, besides on account of its being the easiest and surest way of obtaining a good effect. Nor can anything give this result with less trouble and with greater satisfaction, than first a house of good Cinerarias, and then Calceolarias to succeed them ; and when we remember that there are few classes of plants that can compete with these two for beauty and variety and as effective show plants, no one will dispute my plea for houses devoted entirely to them ; and if grown as they should be there are few persons but will prefer them to most others.

Seedling Cinerarias generally produce much handsomer plants than those grown from offsets, although, to perpetuate the true sort, obtaining the plants from offsets must be resorted to. It is sometimes difficult to do this, for generally the Cineraria will flower itself to death, nor can you prevent it with some sorts ; no one can control the freedom with which some will flower.

No stopping of the growth must be done to Cinerarias with a view to produce offsets. They will not
bear the stopping of the flower scapes ; therefore those
who want to produce plants in this way had better let
the plants flower as they will, and when the signs of
flowering begin to decrease remove them from the
house to a cold shady pit or frame, where probably a
greater inducement will be given them to produce offsets. As soon as these appear, which spring from the
surface of the pot, close to the stems, and when they
are large enough, take them off with a root if possible
attached to each, and pot them into three-inch pots in
a compost of one half fine sifted leaf-mould, and one
half maiden loam with a little sand added, and then
set them in a shady cool pit or frame, giving them
some water. These must be shifted into six-inch pots
as soon as the small pots are filled with roots, and then
they may be continued in the frame or pit, giving an
abundance of air both night and day. Or they may be
set on ashes under a north wall till October, when they
must be placed in the house. If extra fine plants are
required they should be shifted into eight-inch pots at
once from the small ones.

Seedlings must be raised from seed sown annually
in June in seed-pans or under hand-lights in a shady
border, and in soil as described above ; potted off as
soon as they have made six or eight leaves, and treated
in the same manner as for the offset plants, frequently
syringing them all along through the summer, and
continuing it daily till they are in flower. This is the
secret of growing the Cineraria free from insects, mildew, &c. which are so often complained of. Nothing is
required to keep them clean and healthy but daily

syringings with clean soft water, with now and then a fumigating with tobacco in the evening, and syringing in the morning, till they are in flower, then the syringing should be discontinued. As soon as the flower heads are well formed give a weekly watering with weak liquid manure—half an ounce of guano to one gallon of water is quite strong enough. The Cinerarias will all have done flowering by the month of April, when they should be removed from the house and the stages cleaned, and then the Calceolarias may be brought in.

It is infinitely better to grow Calceolarias (I mean herbaceous Calceolarias) in a cool pit or deep frame all along from the seedling stage till they are in their flowering pots and are actually sending up their flower stems, than it is to coddle them in a greenhouse all the winter, where they become infested with insect pests. I have found that they are not at all liable, or at least half so liable, to insects when grown in cold pits till April, as when they are subjected to fire heat. The plants will carry a luxuriant foliage completely covering the pot and will be more robust when in flower ; these will succeed the Cinerarias admirably and make a most unique show for many weeks, and if of good exhibition varieties they will exceed most plants in richness of colour.

The herbaceous Calceolarias cannot be multiplied by any other means than that of seed, which should be sown in the month of May, for flowering the following May ; the seed should be sown on the surface of seed-pans filled with fine leaf-mould, maiden loam and sand, and set in a shady place in a house or pit, and the seed-pan covered with a flat square of glass till the seedlings appear, when air must be given. If the soil is made firm before sowing the seed, and then watered with a fine rose waterpot so as to soak through the soil in the pans, and the seed is then sown over the surface thinly, no water will be required before the seedlings are up.

After the Calceolarias have done flowering, they may be succeeded by a stand of Balsams, which, if good double ones, will pay well commercially speaking ; or, if grown for pleasure, a miscellaneous collection of these with Cockscombs and Fuchsias may succeed them.

This house will hold about 800 Cinerarias, the same number of Calceolarias, about the same of Balsams, and a thousand or more of miscellaneous plants according to the size of them.

# CHAPTER XII.

## THE GENERAL PLANT FORCING HOUSE.

As a rule most people, both amateurs and professionals, find it necessary to force various sorts of flowers, shrubs,

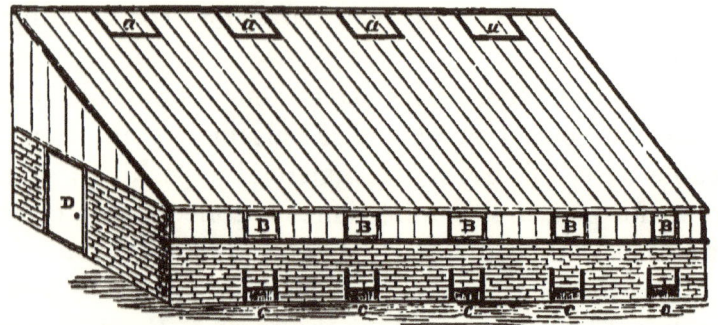

FIG. 26.—SECTION OF A MISCELLANEOUS FORCING HOUSE.
Forty feet long, eleven feet wide, thirteen feet high at back, five feet high in front.

END SECTION OF HOUSE, SHOWING PIT AND PIPES.

References to house.—*a a a a*, top ventilators, to open by cords and pulleys; B B, sliding sashes in front; *c c c c*, zinc shutters, to slide up and down to admit air when the front sashes cannot be opened; D, doorway; E, double set of hot-water pipes; *f*, the tan bed, for plunging pots of flowering shrubs, &c.; G, the pathway all round.

and roots in the same house. For a good compact place for an amateur or a man having a small business the above house is well adapted where a moderate quantity of cut flowers is required. This house is thirty-two feet long, eleven feet wide, twelve feet high at the back, and five feet high in front; the construction, cost, and utility of it are worthy of notice for either an amateur or a professional.

The total cost of this structure by a nice calculation is not more than 61*l*. 4*s*. everything complete, and double-glazed also with fast top clips on the vertical bar, with a good and powerful heating apparatus, pit, and front staging, and everything as is shown. It will take 1,586 bricks for the outer walls except the back wall, 1,719 bricks for the pit, 1,100 feet of 21-oz. glass, 1,080 clips for glazing, and a 30*l*. heating apparatus, &c. &c., the materials to be of the very best kind, and the work equal to any in a plain way. Ornamental work contributes to appearance only, and is all very well for setting off a mansion or dwelling house, and perhaps may be necessary in some cases, but plants will not grow any the better for ornamental work, and it is three times the expense, and, I may safely say, depreciates much sooner than solid plain work.

The cost of such a house complete, if constructed by most of the common builders, will not be one shilling less than 110*l*. or 120*l*. I have no doubt that if any one simply sends the dimensions of this house to any professional builder of such things, and asks for an estimate, that 120*l*. will be the lowest figure. Not long since I drew a plan, for a gentleman, of a house, and gave the estimate for the construction and glazing of it, which was considerably less than 50 per cent. of the price that one or two professional builders did really give in for the contract ; but he got it done at my price, and done well too; and they can do it if they like, but they want to get fully one half profit out of the thing.

It will be found that this house is a good one for early forcing; if the back wall is made of hollow brick-work it will materially add to the earliness of it (see fig. 5, section of cavity wall). The price does not include the back wall; if one has to be made, by all means build this kind of wall for all early houses and, in fact, late ones too. The house should face the south, and be screened from the cutting east winds, which generally affect all early forcing. It should be well double-glazed, especially for the midland and northern counties, where it is difficult to keep out the long and sharp frosts, and to maintain a growing heat when it is wanted the most.

The pit should be well filled with leaves and stable dung or new tan; but I would caution the reader about the tan, which is much liable to breed a most perni-cious fungus. If therefore tan is used, some plung-ing material must be placed on the top of it, deep enough to let the pots into, say, nine inches; for if it comes up to the top of the pots, you will be dreadfully annoyed with one of the worst kinds of fungus, for it will rapidly spread over the whole surface, and kill everything. It seems to possess a perfectly fleshy nature, which I suppose comes from the skins, as it is similar to putrid flesh; so that the tan should never be allowed to reach the pot, but be trodden tight into the lower part of the pit, and filled up with it to within say a foot of the top; then make up this deficiency with sawdust, cinder ash, or sand for plunging the pots in.

It is necessary before anything is brought into heat that it should be well established in the pots; for, if not well rooted before it is introduced into a strong heat, the flowers will suffer, and the plant will fail. For instance, if a Rose is taken up from the ground in November, and ever so carefully potted, and introduced into heat in December, flowers will come upon the plant, but they will be poor, and the plant will probably die in the end. But if a Rose is thoroughly established in the pot fully six months, or, say, from the spring preceding the winter when it is put into heat, fine flowers and a good healthy plant will be the result. So it is with all flowering shrubs, except such as the hardy Azaleas, Rhododendrons, &c., and some of the herbaceous plants; but then even these should be taken up from the ground with good balls of earth, and carefully potted some weeks previous to forcing. The Narcissus will force moderately by planting the bulbs in the pots, and then introducing them into heat; but they will do much better if treated after the manner of Hyacinths; that is, pot them and plunge them into cinder ash, sawdust, or some such thing, five or six weeks before they are put into heat. No potted flowering plants of a strong feeding nature should be shifted immediately before putting them in heat.

All well-established plants will be benefited by weekly applications of liquid manure after they begin to show flower buds. Too much heat immediately after plants are introduced into a forcing house is not good; those recently introduced should at first be placed at the coldest part for a few days or a week. As much light as it is possible to get should be admitted into all forcing houses where there are flowering plants, especially for the fast-growing herbaceous kinds.    No shading should be done to the house from October until March, and then on very sunny days only.

The lists of good free-flowering plants fit for forcing are numerous, but the one below may serve as a fair guide:—

The Roses of various classes, especially the Chinas.

Azaleas, both Indian and Ghent, and the American sorts.

Rhododendrons of all sorts, which may be taken from the ground.

The Kalmias of various kinds—very beautiful evergreen shrubs.

The Andromeda.

The Lilac, and Syringa or Mock Orange.

The Weigela rosea, and W. nivea.

The Deutzia gracilis, a beautiful pure white.

The Gardenia florida, intermedia, &c.

The Jasminum officinale; it must be established in six-inch pots.

Spiræa japonica: this may be taken from the ground in November, potted, and forced forthwith.

Daphne Mezereum—it may be taken up from the ground with a ball of earth if not too old, potted, and put into heat at once; but the plant will suffer, as the Daphnes are impatient of removal, and take a whole year to re-establish themselves if taken from the open ground.    All these are most desirable shrubs for forcing, being very fragrant.    Daphne indica and Blagyana, Cneorum, Pontica, &c., are all good for forcing, but must be grown in pots for the purpose.

The Calycanthus præcox is a good thing, being very spicy and fragrant, but the flowers are small.

Honeysuckles may be forced if grown in eight-inch pots, and of the last season's growth. They should be well ripened and trained at nearly full length on a wire trellis, or by means of three or four sticks, inserted in the pot so as to form a cylinder, when they may be trained round them.

Nerium, or Oleander, is a splendid shrub to force. This plant requires a strong heat, and an abundance of water.

Magnolia of various sorts.

Genista canariensis, a free and beautiful flowering plant.

Guelder Rose, or Viburnum Opulus. This is a re-markably fine mop-flowered plant, having large balls of white flowers, but it must be grown in pots for the purpose.

Pæonia Moutan is a fine genus for forcing, as are also the herbaceous Pæonias; all of which must be grown in pots for the purpose.

Leucopogon Cunninghamii, a beautiful waxy-white flowered evergreen shrub.

There are likewise a number of other shrubs which may be forced ; besides numerous bulbous and tuber-ous-rooted plants, all of which should be well rooted in the pots before they are subjected to a brisk heat. Some will establish themselves in the pots in the course of a few weeks, while others will require a few months, and some will take even twelve months to do so before they can be introduced into heat. As a rule, all succulent and fast-growing plants, such as Hyacinths, the Nar-cissus, the Spiræas, Lachenalias, Crocuses, Snowdrops, &c. will establish themselves in the pots within two months ; while others, like the Rose, will require from six to twelve months before they can be put into heat. The Honeysuckles, Magnolias, Daphnes, &c., must be grown in pots for the purpose.

After the shrubby classes of plants have done flowering, the hardy ones should be put into a cooler house to ripen the new wood for a few weeks, and then plunged out of doors for the summer; but such as the Indian Azaleas, &c., should be continued in a cool house at least till they have made the terminal bud, when they may be set out of doors for a few weeks, to keep them back. All those bulbs that have done flowering should be set under a north wall, and kept moderately moist till they have matured their new parts. With care, most of the herbaceous and bulbous plants will last many years for forcing if carefully looked after when they are once forced.

# CHAPTER XIII.

## THE BALSAM HOUSE.

FOR commercial purposes it is necessary to devote a whole house, or a large roomy and light pit, to the culture of this fine species of plant. Indeed, I think that, as in the case of most other things, an entire

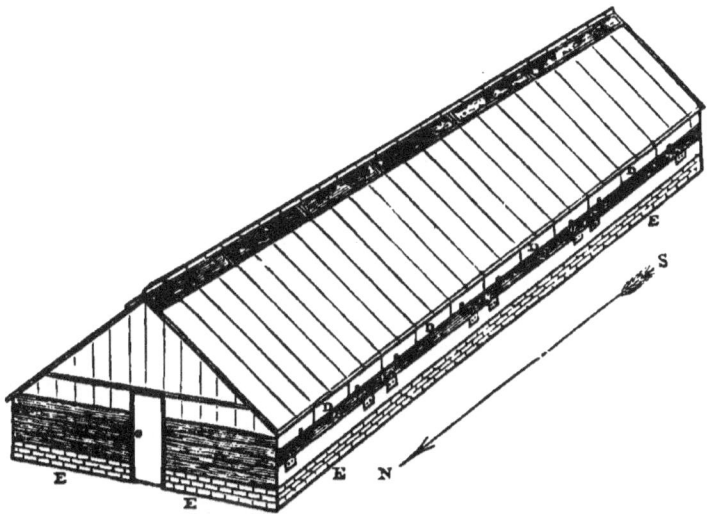

FIG. 27.—SECTION OF A SIXTY-FEET HOUSE FOR BALSAMS, ETC.

Twelve feet high at the ridge, five feet high at the eaves, eighteen feet wide.

References.—*a a*, set of blank ventilators on each side, to open by rack gearing ; B B, set of blank shutters, to open and shut by buttons; D D, one-foot fixed panes of glass all along the fronts ; E E, one foot of four-inch brickwork.

place devoted to the growing of the Balsam is undoubtedly to its advantage, although I have else-

L

where shown that a collection of them can likewise be grown as a successional crop with advantage. But where it is made a special article, it is no doubt a good plan to devote a whole house to it, which, whether for show or seed-saving purposes, should be of a good construction as regards light, room, and air.

Those who may grow Balsams, either for show purposes or for seed, will find that the above plan will be a good one, as well as cheap, to carry out. As it is an annual which can be grown to the greatest perfection from seed sown in March till September, no further security from the weather is required than a careful protection against winds, and the slightly cold nights, &c. The seed must first be sown in seed-pans, and set in a brisk heat till it is well up, and then it may be removed to a cold frame, or to the house, till the seedlings have made from four to six leaves, when they may be at once potted off singly into three-inch pots and kept cool and well watered.

As soon as these are filled with roots, shift them at once into eight- or nine-inch pots, and then keep them close till they have made a full foot of growth, keeping them well watered. Then admit all the air possible, to prevent them from drawing up too much, constantly supplying them with an abundance of water, and once a week give them a watering with some weak liquid manure. It is immaterial what this is, but never give it too strong.

Warrantable double and single seed may be easily saved from the same plant; that is, the seed that will produce none but good double-flowering plants in the next generation may be saved from the main spike of flower, and from the base of the lower laterals; and if it is saved from the extremities of either the laterals or the main spike, none but the commonest single flowers will be the result in the next generation. Mark, learn, and digest this fact, and prove the truth of my remarks. No Balsam seed can be guaranteed to produce double flowers if these conditions are not observed. It is the same with Stock seed, but each can be warranted to produce double flowers—at least ninety out of every hundred will come double—if carefully saved according to these rules; and that is how it is that some customers can be served from the same firm with all good double seed, while others will get, perhaps, not one double flower in five hundred plants. There is no such a thing as changing the constitution of the present seed by cultivation. You can produce as fine-grown specimens of the Balsam as you please by high cultivation, but if the seed is not constituted to produce double flowers by virtue of the concentrated juices of the plant, none, or but a very very small percentage, will come double. Hence the necessity of selecting seed from the main spike, and from the first flowers of the plant. These only are warrantable, and those who save seed otherwise do so at all hazards of reputation.

This careful saving of both Balsam and Stock seed, as well as that of Mangel Wurzel, Beet, Cabbage, Broccoli, &c., is of the utmost importance. In the case of the Balsam and Stock, the flowers should be thinned out, and all except those up the main spike and at the base of the laterals should be taken off, thus concentrating all the powers of the plant in the remaining flowers. This is the only really safe guarantee that can be given for double flowers in the next generation. So much for double Balsam seed saving.

The cost of such a house will be but an item compared with general glass-house building, as no fire heat is required for Balsams after the seed is well up. If the house has a span roof, which is no doubt the best, the plants will then get an abundance of light and air, and sun all round them. It should be set running north and south. My object for this is, that when a span roof is so arranged, each roof gets a due proportion of sun. The Balsams will not occupy the place before May, and at that time of the year a house so situated will get many hours of both early morning and afternoon sun, and the hot mid-day sun, which has a destructive influence upon open flowers, is obviated, although no want of good light is felt. If the house is glazed with eighteen- or twenty-inch squares between the rafters, an abundance of good light, equal to everything that can be desired, will be the result.

The cost may be fairly estimated at 40*l*., besides the staging; and this estimate includes everything else—fixing, painting, brickwork, &c., as follows :—

Eighty-four rafters, four and a half inches by one and a half.

Three hundred and fourteen feet super three-quarter-inch boarding.

Forty-four posts, four and a half inches by three.

Two hundred and forty feet run of plate, four and a half inches by two.

One hundred and forty feet run of fixed sashwork.

Two good ploughed and tongued ledge doors, hinges, locks, and keys.

Sixty feet ridge board.

One thousand three hundred bricks.

Masons' work, and mortar.

One thousand six hundred and eight feet twenty-one-ounce sheet glass, twenty inches by twenty, and carriage two hundred miles.

Six hundred and sixty clips for glazing, and the glazing.

Hinges and ventilating gear.

Total, £40.

This house, if constructed by ordinary builders, will cost, I find, more than 100*l.*

# CHAPTER XIV.

## THE HEATH HOUSE AND CONSERVATORY.

THERE is no class of plants capable of competing with the tribe of Heaths for elegance of character, sub-

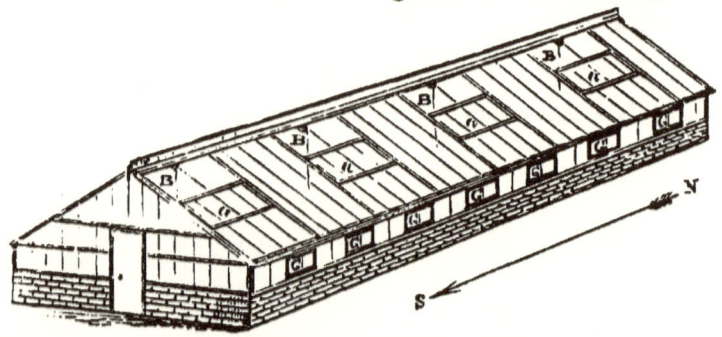

FIG. 28.—SECTION OF HEATH HOUSE.

Forty feet long, twenty feet wide, twelve feet high to ridge, five feet high at eaves.

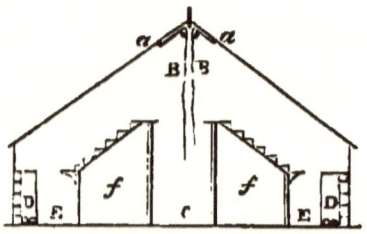

END SECTION OF HOUSE.

References to house.—*a a a a*, sliding sashes, worked by the cords and pulleys, B B B, on both roofs of the house; *c*, the passage under the stand left to come at the cords, to open and shut the house; D D, the hot-water pipes; E E, the pathway; *f*, the stage; G G G G G, sliding sashes; S N, position of house.

stance of flower, variety in colour, and continuation of the flowering season, considered as a tribe. There is no month in the whole year when the Heath may not be had in flower, nor is there a colour, or shade of colour that it does not display. There is, moreover, no class of plants capable of assuming such symmetrical and elegant proportions as this, combined with the most beautiful inflorescence, and in such abundance. It is rather curious that the natural distribution of some Heaths seems so different compared with others. The greater part come from South Africa, but they also seem to extend to the north of Europe; whilst but few, or none, are found in either the east or west.

The culture of the Heath is easy enough, yet we find very few persons who grow them. The London growers, however, are noted for the rapid propagation and commercial uses of this family, and it is quite astonishing how soon these market nurserymen will produce Heaths fit for sale. A few remarks with reference to the way in which it is done may be of some use here. About the beginning or middle of February the young and healthy plants of sorts intended to be propagated are introduced into a house where the average heat is 53° Fahr. but not more. The plants are placed near the glass, a low structure being best suited for them, and very soon they give an abundance of young growth; as soon as the young growth has made half an inch, or not more than an inch of wood, take it off with a sharp and fine-edged penknife with a slight heel of wood at the base. Cut this base smooth, and have pots three inches in diameter filled with fine and pure peat.

Now let me remind the reader that bog-earth must not be used, nor any black soil; to ensure good success in Heath growing none but pure peat is to be used.

This is very scarce in some parts, but no one can successfully propagate Heaths with the peat of Dartmoor, nor
with that which has been dug out of boggy places ; the
peat I mean is to be had from Wimbledon Common, but
the best I ever saw or used, is found in Epping Forest
near High Beech. A few sacks of this can be had for
a few shillings. Having the pots one-third filled with
fine broken crocks, and the other part filled up with
peat, and made firm (the peat should not be perfectly
dust-dry but half dry, as this is the proper state in
which to keep it), insert the little delicate cuttings with
a very small pointed, smooth stick all over the pots at
one inch apart and three-eighths of an inch from the
side, so as to admit of a bell-glass being placed over
them which should fit close inside each. A three-inch
pot will hold about a dozen cuttings. Insert them one
half of their length into the soil ; do it very carefully,
and gently press the soil to the base of them, but great
care is needed in handling the tender cuttings or they
may be bruised, which would cause a failure.

Having filled a pot with these cuttings, give it a
gentle watering with a very fine rose water-pot, and,
after allowing the cuttings to dry off, place the glass
over them, and then plunge the pots nearly up to the
rims in a tan bed that is half spent, or over a very
mild tank, avoiding a greater bottom heat than 50°, as
they will not bear much heat ; the glasses must be
taken off and wiped dry every morning and then be
replaced ; strong sunlight must be avoided. If all
things are as they should be, these cuttings will have
struck root in the course of three weeks, when the bell-
glasses may be taken off, and in the course of a week
more they may be potted off into thumbs ; but care is

necessary to know that the cuttings are all well rooted before entirely taking off the glasses, and before attempting to pot them off. A cool pit or house is best for them after they are well rooted and they are potted off.

Keep all Heaths moist at the root, but never give them water while they are moist just for convenience, that is, do not give them water if they do not require it because you happen to be going away to-morrow, or because you want to go home, thinking to yourself, ' If I do not give them some water now they will be too dry by to-morrow,' as is often the case with persons who have the care of plants. It may do no great harm in the case of Fuchsias, Geraniums, &c., but in Heath grow-ing injudicious watering will prove fatal as surely as you attempt it. But if, on the other hand, Heaths at any stage of their growth are allowed to get thoroughly dry at the root, there remains no remedy ; if they are supersaturated with water equal failure will ensue.

Heaths will not stand too much fire heat, nor must the frost be allowed to reach them ; a damp, close and confined air will also be injurious, as it will surely bring mildew ; sufficient moisture at the roots with frequent overhead syringing during the summer, and an abund-ance of air with partial shade from the sun, these are the necessary conditions for Heath growing.

In the case of large specimens, progressive shifting is necessary, and good drainage with frequent stopping are essential to obtain fine and healthy plants ; but the time of flowering of each species must be observed for the discontinuing of the stopping. Stopping or the nipping out of the points of the leading shoots must be done immediately after the flowering is over, and onwards

till within three months of the flowering; the soft-
wooded sorts soon form the most noble specimens by
frequent shifting and stopping.

I have no doubt about the above house being found
a good one for Heath growing at a very moderate cost.
It will be seen that I have arranged this house to be
set running north and south, which will be found better
than a full south or north aspect, as no direct mid-day
rays of the sun can come on the plants, while the cool
breezes of the west will be admitted to them by opening the sashes on that side.    The cost of this house
may be put at about 80*l.* including everything.

### *THE CONSERVATORY.*

A greenhouse may be, and frequently is, called a
conservatory, but a conservatory is not a greenhouse.
The conservatory is a structure where plants are ex-
hibited or where they are in flower; a greenhouse is a
structure where plants are grown for flower and nursed
till they are in flower, when they are generally brought
into the show-house or conservatory.    However, the
latter may be made a place for the permanent growth of
some plants where they can make progress and display
themselves to greater perfection than they could in a
greenhouse.

Conservatories of various kinds are to be found all
over the country, and some very capacious ones are to
be met with.    There was one (and no doubt it is still
there) at Cashiobury Park, the seat of the Earl of Essex,
which would allow of a coach and four being driven
through it; and that at the Crystal Palace is a fine
specimen of what a conservatory can be made.

A conservatory should be roomy and airy, and so constructed that the full blaze of a summer sun can be prevented from playing upon the plants without artificial or temporary shading; for shading is not good for them except it is of a natural kind, that is, being merely of a nature to weaken the strong rays of the sun. A house set like the one above will answer this end in a great measure. Canvas shading of glass houses is both troublesome and expensive; some thinly clothed creeper or climber may be better used for the roof of a permanent conservatory—such things as the Tacsonia Van Volxemii, Kennedya Marryattæ, Convolvulus mauritanicus, Clematis indivisa, &c. These, if attention is paid to them in training, may be made very useful in merely breaking off the full blaze of a hot sun.

Ornamental conservatory construction is most expensive, and is all very well in some places, and also desirable; but these ornamental places will not grow the plants of themselves, nor will they make a bad gardener a good one; while, in the case of such a plain construction as the one given above, if attended to by a good gardener, its plainness will be lost in the flowery decoration of the interior.

# PART III.

## *THE EARLY FORCING OF VEGETABLES.*

## CHAPTER I.

### FORCING THE POTATO.

It is high time for us Englishmen to rouse ourselves to more energy, and to try and meet the competing foreigner. Now that glass is so cheap, and the cost of construction considerably lessened by glazing without putty, which any man can do, let those who have to get their living by growing early and late market stuff consider whether they can or cannot fairly compete with the Frenchman. Some men are doing this already, but why not all? I think it is very unfair to allow the foreigner to supply our markets when we could, by a little perseverance, do all that is wanted. If early Potatoes will pay them to send here, why will it not pay us to grow them, and get them to market as soon as they do? Of course I know that some little expense at the outset is necessary, but then this is but once. I am now going to show that early Potatoes (as early as those imported) can be as easily grown, and pay as well, as anything else.

Potatoes will not stand much bottom heat, but a good surface heat is necessary to bring them on  Now I will suppose the reader has a good south wall—a brick wall, no doubt, is the best—with space sufficient to form a good border seven or eight feet wide.  On this wall I propose to erect glass, and on the wall to

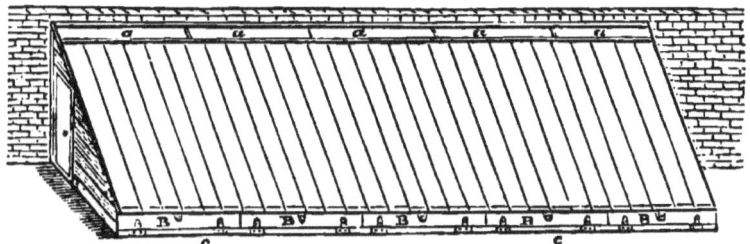

FIG. 29.—SECTION OF A TWO-HUNDRED-FEET POTATO FORCING HOUSE.

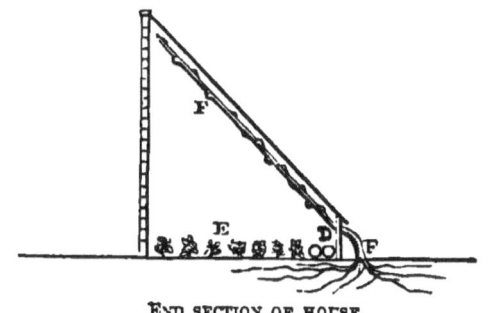

END SECTION OF HOUSE.

References.—a a, sections of top ventilator, opened by rack gearing; B, sections of front flap shutter, hinged below, c c; D, hot-water pipes; E, potatoes; F, grape vines.

plant peaches or plums, and on the border to plant the early Ash-leaved Kidney Potato quite thickly, i.e. nine inches every way.  First fill the ground with leaf-mould only, or dig the Potatoes in, first planting the sets on the bottom of the trench, afterwards put six inches of fine leaf-mould upon them all along the trenches as you proceed.  Plant whole sets, which should be started well before they are planted.  This

is easy enough to do by keeping the sets in a warm
cellar or house a month or two before the planting
time comes, which should be by Christmas.

This house should be furnished with a hot-water
apparatus; one flow-and-return pipe is all that is required, and will be found enough to force Potatoes.
Now if the glass comes down to the ground within one
foot, so much the better; and if the wall is ten feet
high at the back, the glass may reach up to the top
with advantage. This will then be at the angle indicated in the above plan. This pitch of the angle will
give a twelve-feet rafter, which will be a moderate
length for Grape vines, and these would be even
better than Peaches on the wall, because I know that
it is not good to disturb the border much on which
Peaches are growing; and the manuring and cultivation and top-cropping of the border will not at all
injure the vines, but, on the contrary, do them good.
As a permanent crop the vines will pay well, for as
some fire heat must be kept on for the Potatoes, they
will get forward some weeks before vineries with no
fire heat. One vine will carry three rods each for
spurring.

Suppose, then, the whole border eight feet wide by
any length—say two hundred feet—is planted with
Potatoes all over as suggested, i.e. nine inches apart,
planting them six inches deep, then no earthing up
will be required, so long as the ground is made very
fine at the time of planting, and the sets are well
covered with fine old leaf-mould. I do not mean that
which is perfectly decomposed, but leaf-mould from
leaves laid up one year, which will then be sufficiently
decayed for the purpose, and which contains nutriment

enough to produce the very best quality of Potatoes, free from disease, clean and good.

Now I reckon upon two pounds of new Potatoes to every square foot throughout the whole border, for the leaf-mould will produce them nearly all of one size, and rapidly too. Two pounds to every square foot of the border would be five hundred and forty pounds weight per rod or perch, and if the border contains one thousand six hundred square feet in it (that is, nearly six perches of ground), that will be three thousand two hundred pounds weight of Potatoes from the border annually, which would be ready for market by the beginning of May, at, say, 6d. per pound. That is 80l. exactly; yet I am of opinion that this is not an over-estimate, because if they are treated as I have said, I see no reason why two pounds of saleable new Potatoes should not be obtained from every square foot of the border, and they would certainly realise 6d. per pound if they were as good and fine as they could possibly be had. But allowing a good margin for less produce, and net proceeds of say 20l., even then we have a good remunerative balance in favour of the grower.

Then there is the crop that can be had from the same border after the Potatoes are off, which may consist of ridge or hardy frame Cucumbers, and these would really require nothing more than planting and well watering with clean water, and a weekly one with some liquid manure. An abundance of fine Cucumbers would be obtained from this border through the summer. Afterwards come the Grapes, which, at the lowest figure, might be put at one thousand pounds, to sell at 1s. per pound. Thus I can see, and I want others to see too, that it is a speculation quite worth the while for any man to go into with spirit, and one which will enable our home gardeners to compete successfully with the foreigner, and to keep the trade at home.

A fortnight previous to taking the Potatoes up, keep them as dry as it is possible to do. This will give them a nice flavour.

The cost of the construction of such a glass house is not half so much as what some may suppose. I find, by a fair calculation, that this wall structure will cost about 107*l.* 8*s.* But if you go to the profession to get it done, they will charge not less than 197*l.*, and from that to 210*l.*, for the same class of glass and of the same dimensions. Here, then, is a saving of nearly 50 per cent. at the least, and the cost of the house is more than covered by the produce the first season—at least I calculate so—by means of the Potatoes and Cucumbers. Nor do I think anyone will be disappointed, if the thing is well done.

The above estimate includes four hundred feet of three-inch hot-water pipe; one flow and one return pipe, close to the front; and a good boiler, with the fixing; two thousand four hundred feet of twenty-one-ounce glass; carriage two hundred miles, and glazing with clips; one hundred and fifty-five rafters, three inches by two, twelve feet long; two hundred feet eaves plate; two hundred feet wall plate, four and a half inches by one and a half; two hundred feet run of nine-inch board for top ventilator; hinges and gearing; two hundred feet super of one-inch boarding for front; forty posts, three inches by four and a half, two feet six inches long; two close-boarded ends; two doors, hinges, &c.; and fixing and painting three coats.

# CHAPTER II.

## FORCING PEA FRAMES.

GENERALLY—in fact I may say always, and everywhere —early Peas and Potatoes are earnestly wished for, both by the grower and the consumer. The market gardeners, as well as private gardeners, plume themselves on

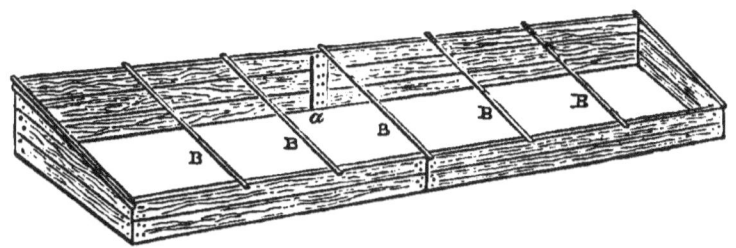

FIG. 30.—SECTION OF A SEVENTY-TWO-FEET PEA FRAME.

Six feet wide, two feet three inches deep at the back, eighteen inches deep in front.

References.—*a*, the nine-inch ledges where the twelve-feet boards meet ; B, the runs for the sashes.

picking the first dish of early Peas in the locality, and of course such are much prized, because Peas at any time are good; but when they can be had a month earlier than is usual, they are more valuable; from 3*s*. 6*d*. to 5*s*. being readily given for the very earliest peck of Peas.

The forcing of Peas consists in growing them under glass without fire heat; and now that glass is very cheap, and the construction of all classes of glass

M

houses is much cheaper than it was, it will no doubt pay well to grow early Peas in this way. If by this means a peck of Peas will realise 10s. instead of 5s., surely it is worth while to grow them under glass.

Frames made of unplaned yellow deal merely nailed together, with sashes fitted to them, would be very inexpensive, and will answer the purpose well. Yellow deals can be bought for 2s. and 2s. 6d. each; these deals are twelve feet long, nine inches wide, and three inches thick. The sawing-down twice will cost 1s., not more, each deal; this makes three boards, making altogether thirty-six feet run of boards, costing 3s. or 3s. 6d. Three depths of these boards, i.e. twenty-seven inches, will be deep enough for the back, and two boards in front, i.e. eighteen inches. Now a frame seventy-two feet long will take six of these deals, costing 1l. 1s. The front will take four, costing 14s.; the ends will take one deal, 3s. 6d.; corner pieces 1s. Two boards will be wanted for broad ledges up the back and the front, where the boards meet to join the frame; nineteen runs for the eighteen sashes. These will take five battens fourteen feet long, seven inches wide, and two inches thick, cut in two, giving the runs three and a half inches wide for the sashes to lie on. The eighteen sashes, four feet wide and seven feet long, will cost 10l.; the making of the frame, nails, and tarring the boards will cost 10s. Thus a frame fit for early Pea culture will come to about 13l.—seventy-two feet long, six feet wide; taking seven-feet sashes, well made and glazed. It is not necessary to plough and tongue the boards, but merely nail them together on ledges and good corner-pieces. The boards will scarcely require planing, as they should be well tarred with coal-tar and

lime ; you may add as much slacked fine lime as you
choose ; the more lime that is added, the thicker will
be the coating and the greater the durability of it.
The tar also gives it a grey colour, according to the
amount put in.

Now if you go to a professional builder of glass-
houses &c. and ask him to make you such a frame, he
will charge you in all about 30*l.* They will be made
better as far as the frame goes, but the sashes are the
same, which is the main thing. These frames are
equal to all that is required for the purpose of Pea
culture. The result of getting Peas in these frames is
encouraging ; and I have no doubt but that, if the
Little Gem is grown in them, from 4*l.* to 5*l.* worth of
pods may be sold in the month of May. When all the
Peas are done with in this frame, it can be used for
Cucumbers, by merely digging up the soil, and turning
in a good lot of rotten manure. The Peas do not cost
much for seed, and give but little trouble.

The Peas should be sown in December, across the
frame, the rows being one foot apart, and the drill one
inch or so apart.

The Cucumbers from this Pea frame will be a remunerative crop. It will take sixty Cucumber plants,
at four feet distant from each other, in patches of three
in the middle of the frame ; each of these clumps of
three will give from twenty to thirty fruit at the least,
if of a good, prolific and hardy sort, such as the Telegraph, Cuthill's Black Spine, or some of the long ridge
kinds ; but either of the two sorts named will do well
through the summer, and produce fruit worth 4*d.* each
wholesale. That would give about 10*l.* for Cucumbers.
So that after the first season a remunerative return

may be realised from this frame without much cost or trouble.

Of course the Cucumbers will require an abundance of water daily; and too much of this cannot be given through the summer. Water them every day, in the afternoon at four o'clock, or at night, and shut up the frames till nine o'clock the next morning, when the sashes may be opened a little, or otherwise, according to the weather: if a hot sun follows the morning, open more; if a cloudy day, not so much. Once a week give the whole of the bed a good watering with some liquid manure, not guano, but such as ' Goulding's special,' not too strong, but rather a little weak than over strong.

Very early Peas may be obtained by sowing them in fine soil, and in a sheltered spot facing the south, and placing over them ridge glasses like those in the illustration below.

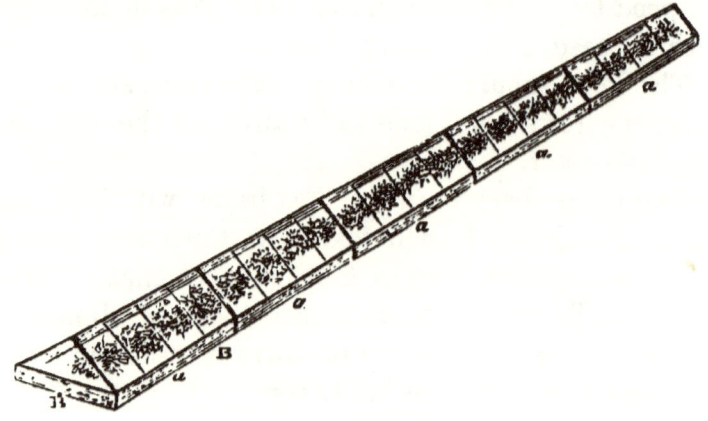

FIG. 31.—SECTION OF TRIANGULAR PEA-GLASSES, IN FOUR-FEET LENGTHS.
References.—*a a a a a*, four-feet lengths; the base board, B, four and a half inches.

These glasses are inexpensive things to make, and are an excellent protection for Peas in rows. They should be two feet every way, *i.e.* two feet at the base across them, and two feet up each roof. They should be made in four-feet lengths for the convenience of removal and for turning them up off the Peas at times, to admit of dressing the crop, and for admitting a day's nice rain occasionally. Blocks must be placed under the south side of the glasses, to allow air to get to the Peas. The glasses may be continued over them till the beginning of May, when they may be entirely removed, and used for ridge Cucumbers, Tomatoes, &c.

The cost of these Pea-glasses will be 6s. for every four-feet run complete, not more. Thus, sixteen feet of glass twelve feet by twenty-four feet, at 2d. per foot, carriage and all, 2s. 8d.; the wood and the making, 3s.; glazing, 4d.; and if painted well they will last for many years. If anyone can make them for himself the cost will be considerably less. Every foot run of such glass will cost from 2s. 6d. to 3s. if made by professional men. The exorbitant prices quoted by high professional horticultural builders are a great drawback to horticulture; they keep back the trade, and admit of the foreigner successfully competing with the home grower. Let the professional market gardener be his own builder, go to the best market for all his stuff, and erect his own glass, and then he will not only save fifty per cent. in the cost, but he will be able to fairly compete with the foreigner. It is even easy for a man to fix his own hot-water apparatus, and it is now a very simple matter for any man to fix his pipes with those india-rubber rings I have before referred to. A mason may be required to set the boiler, but all the rest anyone can do.

# CHAPTER III.

THE Radish as a salad, and for the breakfast-table, is eagerly sought after, especially in the early season. The earlier that Radishes can be had, the more valuable they are.

The Radish is not a very tender plant, but it will not stand frost without suffering in some measure. I have been a grower of early Radishes for many years, and have found that when the frost gets at them, it is a good plan not to remove the coverings till late in the day if the sun shines; but in the case of a continued frost it is more difficult to grow them in the open ground, because the covering of ferns, straw or hay, whatever it may be, must be kept on them, which has the effect of drawing the tops up and turning them yellow; so that whenever they are grown in the open ground they must be covered with five or six inches of one of the above materials, and then this must be removed once in the course of two days.

The best and surest way, however, to get very early Radishes is to build turf pits. These are better than brick pits, or frames, for either early Potatoes or Radishes. The Radish will not bear much top heat, and these turf pits are conducive to a good bottom temperature, and one warm enough for them above, without much covering.

The building of these turf pits can be done by any man. Late in the autumn, say November, cut the turves from a moist place on a moor, or common where the sward is old and tough ; cut them with the turfing iron, a tool well known to gardeners; but as of late some new kinds have made their appearance, I give a sketch below of what I consider the best.

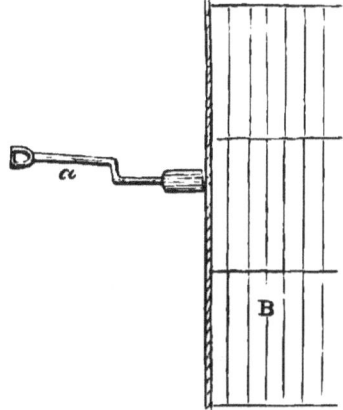

Fig. 32.—The Turfing Iron.

a ; with a section of the turves, lined into three feet by one foot divisions, B.

The crank in this tool brings up the handle to the knee of the man cutting the turves, and obviates the necessity of stooping so low as becomes necessary if no crank is made to it. The operator has more power by this means, by placing the back of the hand holding the handle against the knee, and thus giving the power to drive the tool with ease under the sods ; the blade should be of the best steel, and seven inches long by six wide ; the stem from the blade to the crank should be seven, or not more than eight, inches long; the crank should be five inches deep, set not quite at right angles; the handle must rise from the crank gradually up to the eye of it.

The turves ought to be cut evenly, and it can be done with ease with this tool; both sides of the turf, *i.e.* the edge near to the cutter and the further edge, should be of the same thickness. This may be from two to three inches.

The building of the pits should be done while the turves are thoroughly wet. The grass side should be laid downwards and be well bedded on the one previously laid, carrying the walls upright to two and a half feet at the back, and one foot six inches in front. On the top it will be necessary to lay rough wall plates on which canvas sashes can be fixed. These canvas sashes are made with a frame of light scantling halved and nailed at the corners; on these is tightly stretched some unbleached calico, and tacked on them securely. These canvas sashes should be made in the summer, or at least the material should be dressed over with linseed oil and sugar of lead in the summer, so as to get thoroughly dry and hard. The oil will do by itself, but the sugar of lead dries the oil more quickly and makes it hard; two coats should be given the canvas, which will render it as transparent as is required without the admission of much sun. I have found that these pits and canvas lights are equal to brick pits, and are capital things to keep plants in; while for early Radishes they are first-rate, as no other covering is needed for them.

Radishes may be sown in these pits at Christmas, and will then be fit to draw in March, perhaps by the beginning, if on a warm border, and I am convinced that there is nothing which pays better, if so well, as these things. Plenty of good rotten manure must be forked into the bed, and an abundance of water given them as soon as they get from four to six leaves.

# CHAPTER IV.

## ON FORCING ASPARAGUS, SEA-KALE, ETC.

### *ASPARAGUS.*

I HAVE often thought what a pity it is that Asparagus roots should be thrown away, after giving from 10*s.* to 15*s.* per hundred for them, and after getting perhaps about as much, or a trifle more, from them

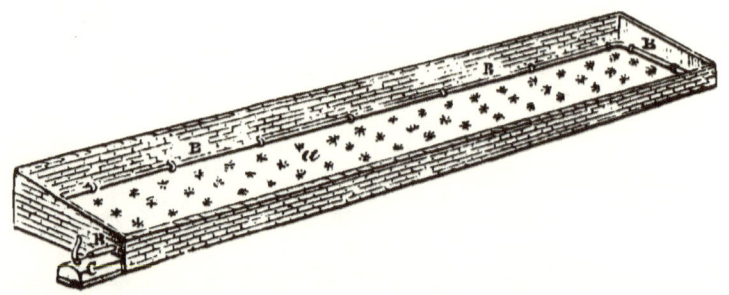

FIG. 33.—SECTION OF A SEVENTY-FIVE-FEET ASPARAGUS FORCING PIT.

References —*a*, the bed, permanently planted with four rows of roots ; B, one flow-and-return three-inch pipe running on the surface of the bed, close to the walls ; c, the boiler.

than what the roots originally cost. Asparagus forcers should remember, that it is not bottom heat that is required to get it early, but a summer heat at the surface. If you plunge a thermometer into a bed in the open ground in the month of April, and shade it, you will find that it will not rise above 40° or 45°; but

if you hang one so that it rests on the surface of the
bed, you will find that it will rise to 55°, and most
likely to 60° in warm sunny weather, when the Asparagus
is growing. This proves that Asparagus only requires
a surface heat, more or less, to get it early.

I propose the setting or building up of brick walls
round established Asparagus beds, similar to the plan
above, but for the purpose of forcing on this plan the
bed should be arranged so as to face the south, with
something to screen it on the north side. If it is
planted three full years before the forcing is begun, so
much the better. Then the four-and-a-half-feet brick
walls may be built two and a half feet high at the
back, and one and a half feet in front. The width
should be eight feet; this will allow of four rows of
roots, and the row next to the walls may then be fourteen inches from them, and the other rows can be a
little less than eighteen inches apart, the plants being
eighteen inches in the rows.

The same preparations which are generally required
in making permanent beds in the open ground are
necessary here. The chief thing in making Asparagus
beds is to dig in as much sea-sand as possible. There
is nothing like an abundance of this, with some seaweed buried in the bottom for Asparagus growing, and
as much pig dung as can be well worked into the soil.
The bed should be trenched eighteen inches or two
feet deep. Every October or November, the surface
should be top-dressed with strong manure, which has
had some pounds of salt, or decomposed seaweed,
mixed with it.

The forcing may begin in January, by putting on a
slow fire, just enough to create a slight elevation of

the thermometer, above the outside temperature, for a fortnight. Keep the sashes close. In the course of a fortnight the thermometer may rise to 60° and then to 65°, at which it may stand, with a rise of 10° during sunny days. Keep the sashes closed, water with tepid water, and sow some salt over the bed once or twice. This will wash in, and help the Asparagus. It will be necessary to treat the beds in the usual way before commencing to force, viz. fork the surface over, and then rake it off fine, so that the heads may come through freely. It is necessary to stop cutting before the plants get exhausted; the cutting must not therefore be continued too long, and the heat may be discontinued as soon as it is done, air being then admitted. It will be advisable in frosty weather to cover the sashes with mats. If the roots are not driven beyond their strength, the bed will last many years.

A small elliptic boiler of twenty-four inches will heat a pit of one hundred feet long, costing 2l. 3s. The two hundred feet of three-inch pipe will cost 7l. 10s. carriage and all; four elbows, at 2s. 8d. each, 10s. 8d. The fixing of the boiler, bricks, &c. will cost 2l.; the india-rubber rings for fitting the pipes, 5s. per pound. Here then is a good, simple, and effective apparatus for sufficiently heating such a pit for a little more than 10l. The cost of the pit, sashes, &c. may be compared to the Melon pit, frames, &c.

### SEA-KALE.

Many methods are adopted to get early Sea-kale, but I know of none to equal covering up the roots where they stand. Sea-kale will not bear a great dry heat. The heat of a forcing house, however moist it is kept, does not suit Sea-kale; under such circumstances it is wanting in crispness and solidity, and the tops only are nice and tender when cooked. But when it is forced, by covering it first with pots and then with fresh-gathered leaves of the same fall of the year, the Kale is of quite a different quality, being solid, crisp, and rich, in which case all of it may be cooked and eaten to the extent of five or six inches in length.

There is nothing to equal leaves for forcing this vegetable. Hot and fresh stable dung, if put on of a thickness sufficient to cover the pots well, will ferment to a scalding heat, which will last for a week or two and then decline, and the heat will have all passed off without the least benefit to the Kale, for it will not have made the least progress while the manure was hot. Sea-kale will not force, to be fit for anything, under six or eight weeks from the time that the dung is put on the roots. I have tried it, and therefore can vouch for what I say. But leaves act differently if they are put on the covers, filling up the spaces as well, and forming a bed over the whole of the plantation.

It is much the best and most economical to make Sea-kale plantations consisting of not less than three rows, i.e. three rows three feet apart and three feet from plant to plant. It is far better to make the plantation in a square of three rows than to plant one row only through a quarter; for then, when the fermenting material is put on the pots containing the roots, it forms a solid bed, which makes the best of the heat. The leaves will maintain an equal heat for many weeks

in succession if, when they are put on, they are trodden
well among the pots, filling up all the spaces, and if
the leaves are wet they will work in very close and
form a lasting heat for the whole of the time required
for the Kale. I have found that it is considerably the
better when forced by leaves than by stable manure.
Leaves can be raked up during November, and put on
at once.

It is better, in my opinion, to plant but one of the
kind, if strong, for a smaller pot, than to plant three
crowns in one place for a large pot. Or three crowns
may be placed quite close together, instead of five or
six inches apart, in an angle, as is more usual. I have
found that when they are so planted the crowns invariably get beyond the limits of the large-sized pots,
and generally come outside it, or just under the rim.
One good strong root is enough for a pot, and some
sea-sand should be dug into the soil when a plantation
is made, and the whole space in which the pots are
should be covered with three inches of sea-sand, completely covering the crown of the plant. This will keep
down slugs.

Some preparation is necessary before forcing time
comes on. In the course of the summer go over the
crowns and thin them out, leaving no more than three,
which should be the strongest. If this is not done
there will be a crowd of spray crowns, which will give
poor Kale, pithy and small stuff. Good bold crowns,
are what is wanted to produce a fine vegetable; three
of such crowns to each pot are enough. There is no
doubt but that the very best Sea-kale may be produced under such circumstances, and that the poor,
pithy, and insipid kind which we see at times is grown

under different conditions; that is, from housed and small roots, with too much dry heat, &c.

## RHUBARB.

The same plan may be adopted in forcing Rhubarb, for this, like Sea-kale, will not bear a very strong and dry heat; covering it precisely in the same manner as for Sea-kale will be found to answer best. The roots should be three- or four-year-old well-established plants. Before covering up the pots containing the crown, give the whole of the ground a soaking with guano and soot; put, say, two pounds of guano in a tub holding twenty gallons of water, and add five or six pounds of soot, then stir it well, and water the ground where the roots are. This will induce the crowns to break very strong. About the beginning of the month of December, Rhubarb may be set to work. It is a plant of hardy constitution, and may be handled roughly, but good roots are often sacrificed by driving them too sharp when they are subjected to a strong dry heat.

If Rhubarb is forced in the same way as Sea-kale, much finer stuff will be had, and no sacrifice made as regards the roots. When it is forced otherwise they should be strong, for only poor thin stuff is got from small roots. Rhubarb should be taken up and replanted every four or five years, for if you want to prevent it from running to seed, the roots must be replanted about those periods. The best time to do this is in the month of October. Turn out the whole root, divide it into single crowns, trim off the lacerated roots to a solid part, and then replant them.

Frequently Rhubarb, although always required early and good, is planted in some out-of-the-way corner, and very often close under a hedge. This is a mistake. Plant the roots in as warm a spot as you can find, for the sake of getting early growth, but never put it near hedges, trees, or strong-feeding shrubs. One season it may be moderately fine, but after that it will get less and less, till, in the end, it will not produce stuff larger than the finger.

# CHAPTER V.

## THE CARROT.

EARLY and young Carrots are sought for and are thought much of, and deservedly so; for, let old Carrots be what they may, they have lost that delicious and fine flavour which they had when as large as the finger, as well as the fine texture they then possessed. To get very early Carrots, some means must be devised beyond that of a warm border in the open ground. The same class of frame as I recommend for early Peas (fig. 30) may be used, but some preparation of rather a different kind must be resorted to.

A moderate-sized bed must be made with leaves, tan, or cocoa-nut refuse fibre. Leaves raked up in November are as good as anything for forcing Carrots. The next best material is tan, which suits the Carrot well, and a bed made with it, two feet and a half thick, well trodden down as you proceed, will last in a nice heat as long as it may be required. The bed may be made in December, but before sowing the seed some four or five inches of fine light soil must be put over it, in which the seed should be sown. It will be a good plan to put five or six inches of old tan over the new tan first, and then the fine earth, for I find that new

N

tan is very liable to produce a most destructive fungus, which I have mentioned before.  If, therefore, some old tan is first put upon the new bed, and then the earth, no fungus will get through to the surface of it.

It is as well to let the heat rise before sowing the seed, as it is best for Carrot seed to be stimulated to cause quick germination.  The surface soil should be fine and half dry, and should it get quite dry, a light sprinkling may be done in the morning with a fine rose waterpot.  As soon as the seed is well up, which will be in the course of a fortnight, admit a little air by day. If cold nights come on, lay mats on the sashes, and if sharp frosts ensue, first cover the sashes with dry hay and then a mat.  The Short-horn and James's Intermediate Carrot will be the best sorts for this purpose.

When the Carrots are drawn, some soot and salt may be sown over the bed, in the proportion of one pound of salt to three or four pounds of soot well mixed for each perch of ground, and well worked into the soil for five or six inches deep, and the Carrot seed sown a second time.  This will probably be about March when young Carrots will be obtained a second time from the same bed, long before any can be had from the open ground.  Soot and salt are no doubt the best manure that can be had for Carrots, and for the open ground two pounds of salt to the same quantity of soot may be used.

### DWARF FRENCH BEANS

To get this desirable vegetable early whenever it can be accomplished is no doubt the great wish of most persons.  The term 'forcing' may be classed into two or three divisions. There is what we call driving things—this class of forcing is not always within the reach of many. Then there is a medium kind of forcing by which all who possess glass may have early Beans. And there is also another way to get early Beans in frames and pits without fire heat. To force dwarf Beans in the first manner, a good brisk heat is necessary, such as is applied to early vineries. The second class of forcing consists in sowing Beans in pots and placing them in a warm greenhouse ; and as I have said early Beans may also be had by sowing them in the ground in a frame.

It is astonishing with what rapidity Beans come on under glass, nor is there a vegetable that pays better to force. I am convinced that every respectable family which can command a little ordinary glass will not only be gratified by the experiment, but also satisfied that a frame devoted to early dwarf Beans is not lost : an ordinary close common-made frame with sashes will do well for this purpose ; such a one as I have described and illustrated for Peas (see fig. 30) will be a good one for these; and if you want them very early the Asparagus pit (fig. 33) is just the thing. This last will be found fit for anyone who wants to get very early Beans ; the advantages of this heated pit will soon be seen. The Beans are sown in the bed, which should be of a good rich and light nature, consisting of common garden soil well manured, and if not light enough, it should be made so by the addition of some leaf-mould. The soil of the bed should be manured and forked up some time before sowing, so that the surface may be made fine and light. Sow the seed in drills across the bed one foot six inches apart, or perhaps one foot three inches will do if some of the dwarfer sorts are wanted. Zion House and Fulmer Early are the best free-bearing and dwarf sorts to grow for any class of forcing.

For high-class forcing the Beans should be sown three in an eight-inch pot of old hot-bed manure and maiden loam of equal parts, giving a good drainage to the pots. They should be placed in a Cucumber house or early vinery, but it is necessary in order to be really successful, to get as much light as possible to them in the early season, so as to get an abundance of large Bean pods, and for this purpose a good house is necessary for them where a brisk and lively heat can be kept up, and where the pots can be placed near the glass. It is best to fill the pots about two-thirds with a compost (making it moderately firm), and then to place the Beans in an angle on it, covering them one and a half inches with half dry, light and fine soil—leaf-mould two parts and maiden loam one part. Give no water till the seed is up, and not much then. As the plants get strength and grow above the pots, fill them up among the Beans with half-dry compost; be careful of watering too much till the plants get strong and begin to show fruit, when more may be given, and as soon as the pods begin to come on freely, give some weak liquid manure for a few times.

Beans are liable to the attacks of the red spider, when the atmosphere is too hot and dry; so that frequent syringing must be resorted to to prevent them, and while the Beans are growing freely fumigation will prevent the attacks of this pest.

# CHAPTER VI.

In some localities the chief difficulty in getting Mush-rooms by artificial means is the liability of this fine sauce vegetable to be attacked by that insidious enemy the woodlouse (*Oniscus*). This enemy of the Mushroom

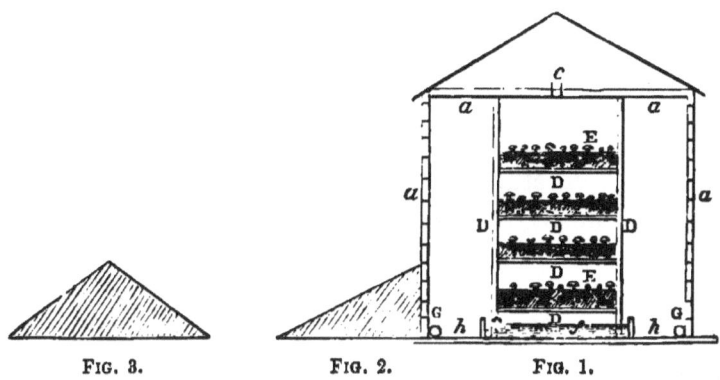

FIG. 3.          FIG. 2.          FIG. 1.

FIG. 34.—END SECTIONS OF MUSHROOM HOUSE AND OUT-DOOR MUSHROOM BEDS.

References.—Fig. 1: *a a a*, outer walls and ceiling of house; *c*, the ventilator; D D D, the framework of the beds; E E E E, the beds; *f*, bed of cold water for vapour, and to prevent the woodlouse and beetles getting to the mushrooms; G, one flow-and-return three-inch pipe, for heating the house; *h*, the pathway. Fig. 2 : Lean-to out-door bed. Fig. 3 : Span-roof out-door bed for summer work.

grower is hard to avoid in wooded, rocky, and dry districts. It is most remarkably fond of the Mushroom, and commits its depredations while the gardener is asleep. To get Mushrooms in such places more than ordinary means must be resorted to; but old cellars and

Mushroom houses at the back of hothouses in localities infested by this pest will always prove futile for
complete success, unless some additional provision is
made to keep off these marauders.   It is much better
in such localities to go to the expense of building a
Mushroom house quite independent and detached from
all other buildings, so that in extreme cases there may
be no harbour to encourage these pests more than can
be well avoided.   They will, I know, find their way if
possible, to any rendezvous where they can get the
warmth, seclusion, and food that they like; but they
are rather careful not to expose themselves too much,
lest they may get picked up by an enemy and be eaten.
And here let me give a little of what I think timely
and valuable advice.   In such localities as I refer to
where the woodlouse naturally abounds, let intending
Mushroom growers get as many hedgehogs and guinea
pigs as they can and keep them about the place.
Hedgehogs! say some : how are you going to keep
hedgehogs?   Why, keep them in the Mushroom house,
to be sure, where they will destroy every beetle and
woodlouse, and the guinea pigs will do the same work
outside.

The Mushroom house should be so constructed as
to prevent the intrusion of the woodlouse.   In the
first place the outside walls must be proof against the
ingress of all such pests ; and secondly, no beds should
be made on the immediate ground floor, but should be
raised about a foot, so that a trough of water may run
round the floor, as seen in the above plan; this will
prevent them from climbing the walls and the stays of
the beds above.   The woodlouse will not enter water.

The troughs of water will give off a congenial vapour

favourable to Mushroom culture, and prevent that poisonous and dry atmosphere which generally attends these houses. It is a recognised fact that the species *Agaricus campestris* becomes poisonous, more or less, according o the state of its surroundings. Let any one get Mushrooms fresh gathered from our rich open pastures, and some also from a dry Mushroom house, and cook both lots separately ; serve them up, and have the unprejudiced opinion of those who taste them ; and I know that the most decided favour will be given to those gathered from the pasture. It would be quite impossible to get a Mushroom to retain that purity and richness at the size to which they grow in the meadows from an ordinary Mushroom house. Why is this ? Not solely on account of the soil, for generally a made bed contains considerably more manure than a meadow. No, it is chiefly on account of the dewy state of the atmosphere which prevails at night during the Mushroom growing months, September and October. It is this which gives purity and richness of flavour to the Mushroom. The water troughs on the floor of the house will answer two most important purposes, viz. prevent the ascension of the woodlouse and beetles to the beds, and cause the necessary vapour for the production of really good Mushrooms.

No difficulty stands in the way of having Mushrooms all the year through, if a convenient house like the one in the illustration is built. They may then be grown without houses for nine months of the year. To have them in June it is necessary to make a bed under some warm and sheltered wall or hedge, in the month of March or the beginning of April. Having chosen a favourable spot, commence by digging out the soil a foot deep and five feet wide, and of any desired length. Turn the soil out on one side, if good; and then, having a sufficient quantity of well-fermented manure ready, commence to make the bed. But before that is done fill up the space which has been dug out with some brushwood or faggots—not, however, quite to the outside, but from the back to within a foot of the front edge. On this brushwood or faggots place the dung—stable dung it should be—tread, and beat it firm as you proceed, so as to ensure a solid bed of fully two feet in depth, and then rake the surface over, and beat it with the back of the spade as a finish.

The bed, if against a wall, should be at a moderately sharp lean-to pitch (see fig. 34); but if on an open spot it may be made a sharp span-roof. The manure or dung must not be over-fermented, *i.e.* not exhausted in its fermenting power, but half done. When the bed is made, break up the soil turned out of the trench below and make it as fine as you can with the spade. It should be of a somewhat adhesive nature, but not cold or poor clay, nor of a dry dusty kind; good by nature and made good by manure for other crops that have been in the ground; it should also not be too wet. If dust-dry, water it before putting it on the bed; it should properly be half dry, so that it will adhere together when beaten, which it should be finally, so as to form a tolerably smooth surface.

A few sticks as large as the finger should be plunged into the bed a foot deep, to ascertain the heat of it by pulling them out once within twelve hours, and taking hold of the warm end; if the heat is up, and they are as warm as milk just from the cow, immediately put in the spawn; this is best done by the thick end of a hand

dibber. First, make holes two inches deep and one
foot apart all over the bed; then thrust in each hole
a piece of spawn the size of hole, and press it in tight.
Having spawned the bed, place a handful of fine half-
dry soil over each hole, and beat it in with a mallet.
This being done cover the bed over, first with dry old
hay or straw, and then with straw mats, to keep off
excessive wet.

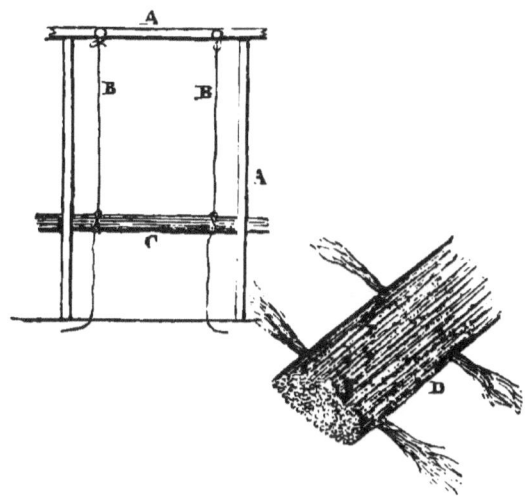

FIG. 35.—SECTION OF STRAW MAT MAKING.

References.—A, the door frame, in which the nails are driven to hold the cords, B ;
c, the first handful of straw tied in ; D, bundle of reed, or straw.

Here I may as well, for the convenience of the
inquirer and those who have never made, or seen straw
mats, just describe them. First, get some straw, called
' reed ' in some places—straw that has not been machine
thrashed, and then some rope yarn or tar twine, and
fasten two long pieces of the twine on strong nails,
each two feet apart, driven into the head of a door
frame. Then take a moderate handful of the straight
straw, keeping the base ends of it quite even, and,

beginning at the bottom, place the first handful the width you intend the mat to be, bring up the twine over the handful of straw, pass the end round the line of twine behind and draw it tight—this ties every handful in tight. Then place another handful of straw of the same size on the last, and tie that, and so on till you get to the top, and the mat will be of the width you wish it. Now with a pair of sheep shears cut off the corn ends of the straw to make the mat straight and even at that end. So the mat is made, and if made well, and tied tightly as you proceed, it will last two or three years. These mats are easily made, are cheap, and far better than Russian mats or any others which are used for covering frames, Mushroom beds, and various other things.

Place these mats like thatch on the Mushroom bed just spawned; examine the bed at intervals of twelve hours to see if the heat is too much or too little; if too much, remove some of the covering for a short time; if too little, put on more dry hay, ferns or straw. If after three weeks from the time the spawn is put in the bed the surface has become very dry, give it a little water without the rose, putting it between the original places where the spawn was introduced, but not too much. In the course of six or seven weeks the Mushrooms will appear. Covering to the bed is necessary, but merely sufficient to protect it from the hot sun, and cold nights. This method of Mushroom growing may be pursued by all who desire to have them at all times, except in the dead of winter.

In the case of growing them in the house, shelves and well-prepared horse droppings are necessary; and thoroughly well-made beds on shelves, which should be

made of close oak or elm boards an inch and a half
thick, or even two inches will not be too much; my
reason for this is, that the beds may not get too dry.
The bottom of the shelves need not be ploughed and
tongued, but merely fitted moderately close, then there
will be sufficient drainage to secure the beds from stagnant damp. These shelves should have side boards
rising from six to nine inches above the bottom. A
small flow-and-return pipe should run once round the
house, to keep the temperature at 55° or 60° during the
winter months. A two-inch pipe will heat a small house
quite enough; and a three-inch pipe is large enough
for any house used for Mushroom growing. As will be
seen in the plan above, I prefer the pipes running round
the walls, instead of in the middle of the house; one
flow-and-return pipe will be ample. Too much heat is
positively detrimental in growing Mushrooms. If we
consider the conditions under which they flourish best
naturally, we find that they do not require a great heat,
but a temperature of considerably less than 50°. Many
a time have I been out early in the morning in the
months of September and October, 'mushrooming' as
we used to call it, when I was young; when it has been
so cold that one would be glad of a great coat, and the
dew has been quite heavy on the grass, like a hoar frost
dissolved, so that my boots have been as thoroughly
soaked as if I had walked in water over the tops, such
has been the condensing power of the cold through
the night. 'Ah!' thought I, 'this is the morning for
Mushrooms,' and so it used to turn out generally. This
should teach us two important things: first, a good dry
heat to spread the spawn; and secondly, a moist and a
lower temperature to grow the Mushroom.

The *Agaricus campestris* will grow to an immense size under favourable conditions. I have gathered them as large as an ordinary dinner plate, at least nine inches in diameter, and so full of catsup that one pint has been made from one of them, and many a time they have been gathered as large as a small cheese plate. I merely note these things to show under what conditions the Mushroom will do best, and to modify the idea that they can be grown by very clever men only. In the plan at the head of this chapter I have no doubt that it will be seen that the water at the bottom of the beds is necessary everywhere in houses where heat is indispensable in order to obtain winter Mushrooms; and, as I have said before, in localities where the woodlouse and beetle abound, it will be a bar to their getting at the beds. It is necessary to thinly but securely cement the trough a little beyond the uprights of the beds, so that the feet of these posts are surrounded by water; or the beds may rest on brick pillars one foot high from the floor of the house.

This house is on a scale of one-eighth of an inch to one foot. This gives four-feet pathways and eight-feet beds, which may be rather wide, but they should not be less than six feet wide; then there is more body in them, and they will not dry so soon. The beds should be not less than one foot thick, and should be well beaten together when made, with a mallet. The droppings from the stable may contain some short straw; all should be well mixed and laid up in a heap to ferment a few days before making the beds, and some half-dry or old cow-dung may be mixed with the droppings when the beds are made. The earthing of them after they are made should be done immediately, and the soil beaten firmly on them, and as soon as the heat rises, put in the spawn. No light is needed in the house for some time, and but little air at any time. A slow fire may be put on in the winter as soon as the spawn is in the beds, so as to keep a nice warmth in the house, but too much heat is not good.

A house like the one above is capable of growing any quantity of Mushrooms all the year round, and would well repay market men. It may be built at a lean-to pitch at the back of a house, but where the woodlouse abounds it is better to build it independent of any other building, and on this principle. The walls, doors, and ceiling should be quite proof against these pests, and the ventilators at the top made secure by nailing perforated zinc over them.

Mushroom spawn may be bought of good quality at 5s. per bushel, but it can be made for less and by anyone; although it is scarcely worth while for anyone except those who grow for the market to take the trouble to make it. These men know how to make it generally, but it may be had in abundance from mill tracks; that is, where corn-fed horses are used to work malt mills and other machinery. In these places it generates, and is of first-rate quality. To have Mushrooms all through the winter months, make beds in the house in October and November, and again out of doors in March for the summer.

# CHAPTER VII.

FEW people are aware how the fine Portugal Onion is produced. The Onion, I well know, requires heat; too much heat can scarcely be given to it; therefore plant or sow it in the best and most favourable spot for the sunshine that you can find. To get the finest Onions, choose some of the large-growing sorts, such as Globe Tripoli, Giant Rocca, or Giant Madeira. Sow the seed thickly on some poor ground exposed to the full influence of the sun about the middle of August; or it may be sown in cold frames quite thick, and induced to form small bulbs, which should, however, be ripened, when they may be pulled up and well dried, as for picklers; but they should be kept in a cold room till March or April when some thoroughly rich ground should be prepared for them in the hottest place you can find; but the ground must be thoroughly good. To make it so, rough-dig it first in the month of February, mark it out into four-feet beds, and then put the contents of the common sewer on the top of them, all over, as a good thick dressing, and let it remain exposed to the full influence of the air. If this is done in January or the beginning of February, the manure will get completely pulver-sed, and lose its injurious qualities.

In the beginning of March or by the middle of the month, go over the beds with a three-pronged dung hook, and work the surface over five or six inches deep, mixing the manure well with the soil, and then leave it for a week, at the end of which rake down the ground with a coarse rake, leaving a fine surface ; and after the first shower that comes dib in the small bulbs in rows across the beds, seven or eight inches apart from row to row, and six inches from plant to plant; do not bury them too deep. These small bulbs will give the earliest and best Onions, but they must not be sown too early, nor allowed to be too thin, or else they will run to seed. As soon as they begin to swell off, and show no signs of running to seed, sow a slight quantity of 'Goulding's Bone Manure,' or 'Goulding's Special,' over them, but mind not to overdo it ; in the proportion of one pound to every thirty square yards will be quite enough. Keep them clean, and clear out the soil round each bulb when they are the size of a breakfast cup ; the bulbs will then swell rapidly, and come to a large size and ripen thoroughly by the month of July. When the tops turn yellow, pull them up and let them lie on the top of the ground to finish off through the power of the sun, which they will do in the course of a week, if the weather is fine. Then they may be trimmed off and sold. By this means the English grower may be able to fairly compete with the French, and by perseverance will have finer Onions ready for market before they can bring them here.

There is still another way by which the English Onion grower can compete with the French for our own markets. Get some seed of Danvers's Yellow, or the Banbury Yellow, and prepare a broad piece of good land well facing the south, and not at all shaded. Dig it and manure it well in the month of July or the beginning of August. Dig it deep, twelve or fourteen inches, make the surface moderately fine, and drill the seed in six inches apart from row to row, and sow the seed thinly if you can depend upon its vitality. If the seed comes up too thick, thin out, as is usual in the case of spring-sown Onions.

In the month of November spread a thick sowing of fine cinder ashes over them, so as to cover the surface; this will prevent the frosts from drawing the young Onions out of the ground, which long and severe frosts are apt to do. In the months of March or April sow over the whole a good dressing of bone manure, about four pounds weight to the rod, hoe it in, and then tread the beds over so as to make the surface firm, and by the month of June or July fine ripe and large Onions will be the result. Let our English market gardeners thus try to meet the home demands and keep out the foreigner. The Onion can be made to meet the early demands at home if either of these plans is adopted. If a suitable spot of land is chosen, and they are grown on a large scale, it can be done; but to follow the ordinary course of sowing Onions in the spring, and running the hazard of an unfavourable summer to ripen the bulbs, is bad policy on our part. Under the most favourable conditions as regards weather, they will not ripen till after our markets are filled with French Onions, which brings down the price so that it does not pay to grow them.

In some of the mild counties of England where the

soil is of a sandy and favourable kind the Onion crop will pay well on a large scale when grown on either of these plans; the land may be ploughed deep two or three times over, well manured, harrowed and made fine, and the seed drilled in, and finally rolled for the seed.

# CHAPTER VIII.

THE importance to be attached to the watering of crops and plants in pots is greater than may be imagined. If any part of gardening operations requires a practical knowledge it is watering. When to water, what to water, and how much water to give, are very important things to be considered; plants often suffer by having too much water given them as well as by not having enough. Watering the plants should be the study of those in charge of them, as doing it indiscriminately often proves fatal. Amateurs frequently come with complaints to the person from whom they purchased the plant, now presenting a sickly appearance, which perhaps has been supersaturated with water, or perhaps merely wetted on the top while the roots are thoroughly dry.

Some plants must be supersaturated with water to succeed well with them, while this treatment would destroy others; and then again the physiological condition of the plant is another thing to be duly considered. Take, for instance, a plant of a gross-feeding constitution: when the roots fill the pot and there is no soil for it to feed upon, sufficient water must be given to enable it to live and perhaps to flower. I know from long experience that many plants will not only live, but even do

well as regards both foliage and flower for many years
without shifting, by supplying them with an abundance
of water ; while on the other hand too much water given
to plants not so circumstanced would cause them to
suffer.

It is not only requisite to know the physical constitution of the plant, but also the circumstances connected
with its root. A plant, for instance, that is well established in the pot, *i.e.* the pot being full of root and the
plant coming into or being in flower, will require more
water than it would when it was first potted into fresh soil
and was in a more inactive stage of growth. As an ex-
ample, a Geranium that has just been cut back and re-
potted does not require half the water that it does when
it begins to show flower. Again, the Cactus is an instance of what is required by way of abundant watering
and then a period.when no water should be given. The
Heath is an instance of careful watering ; too much or
too little will surely prove fatal to it.

The Heath may be considered a safe guide for careful watering, a sort of medium rule in the matter ; and I
think if this tribe was made a sort of criterion in this
respect, no great harm would ever arise from the operation ; for there are few plants indeed but require some
such regular root treatment in watering. There are however some exceptions, and these consist of the Cactus
tribes, the Tydæas, Orchids, Agaves, &c. which require
an entire season of rest, when no water is required,
while on the other hand aquatics always require water
in abundance. Still the Heath may be taken as a rule
for careful watering in general ; but note this : no
plants require half so much water during the winter as

they do in the summer, nor half so much during dull
and sunless days in summer as they do when the sun
bears upon them and in windy weather. Never give
water when the plant is damp; most plants except the
Heaths and some Ferns will bear a little drought; when
they are watered give them enough to soak quite through
the pot, but never (except in the case of aquatics) allow
the saucers to hold the water under the pot longer than
it has drained from the pot after watering.

In the case of watering plants in the ground, one
thing should be observed, and that is, when beds require
water they should have it so as to thoroughly soak the
soil. Never water over the ground a second time during
the same watering; do all that is required for the subjects as you go along, and do not go over the ground
twice at the same time, for you will find that by doing
so the surface gets into a muddy state, and when it
becomes dry it will get baked under the action of the
sun, forming a surface impervious to the air. This
applies to all ground watering among annual crops, bedding plants, &c. For this reason I condemn all those
waterpots that let out the water over large areas by
driblets; they are simply injurious, by first damping the
surface and then working it into a mud pool, which
should be studiously avoided. But the old-fashioned
rose gives out the water over a small area, and by holding the pot pretty close to the surface (as close as you
can), the water can be controlled at pleasure by moving
the hand slowly or quickly in a regular way according
to the quantity required; the watering is thoroughly
done without injury to the soil.

After beds and crops are watered, the next morning
at furthest, they should be lightly hoed over to form

a dusty surface so as to prevent evaporation, and thus avoid the necessity of watering again for some days. If the surface is not hoed it will soon dry, and the watering must be done again much sooner than would be required if the surface was stirred.

# PART IV.

## MONTHLY CALENDAR FOR THE FORCING GARDEN.

For the sake of a ready reference I think a Calendar of operations may be convenient here.

### JANUARY.

THE EARLY VINERY.—In the beginning of the month the house may be fairly started if not already done, and pots of Strawberries may be introduced. French Beans may also be sown in pots (see p. 179), and Rhubarb roots may be introduced and placed in tubs or large boxes, being covered to keep the light from them; a moist heat should be kept in the house.

All vine pruning must be finished or the vines will bleed. When bleeding does occur, stop it at once with some painter's knotting put on with a brush.

THE LATE VINERY.—All pruning should be done at once and the vines dressed over with a thick solution of Gishurst compound, or soft soap, sulphur vivum and soot made into a thick paint. Strawberry pots may now be put into this department and set on the ground floor, and where they are set let them remain for fruiting, as the roots will get through the pots very soon and

get into the border, which will feed them; give little
or no water to them for some time.

THE PEACH HOUSE.—Keep the Peaches as quiet as
possible, but if in pots give water to keep them from
shrivelling. Introduce Strawberry pots. A little ventilation at the top may be given if the weather is mild
and sunny.

THE PLUM HOUSE.—All pruning and thinning of the
spurs should be finished and the house kept cool. The
Cherry house the same.

THE GOOSEBERRY HOUSE.—All pruning should be
finished, and the trees dressed with soot all over. This
will prevent the Gooseberry fly from attacking them, as
it will do, if it has not probably done so already.

THE CUCUMBER HOUSE.—This department will now
require close attention; a good brisk heat of 70° must
be kept up; should the weather be frosty no syringing
must be done. Close attention must be paid to insect
pests, and the remedy applied if the least signs of them
appear (see p. 64). Stopping and training must be
duly attended to.

THE MELON HOUSE.—Some early plants may now be
planted in the pits and a good brisk heat kept up. Be
sparing with the water, and never water these immediately on the root-stems. Pots of Beans and Potatoes
may be introduced.

THE PLANT HOUSE.—As a rule, most of the
inmates of the stove plant-house will be quiet, and
therefore water must be cautiously given. The shrubby
Begonia, Coleus, Gloxinia, Euphorbia, Streptocarpus,
Deutzia, Hoya, &c. must now be carefully watered;
while others, such as the Gardenias, and those that are
moving and coming into flower, may be dealt with

more liberally; but it is safer to err on the right side, and not water too freely at this time, when there is not much sun. Some plants may be shifted and re-potted, and such as are required for early flowering may be introduced. The temperature should be kept on the rise from 60° to 70°.

THE CAMELLIA HOUSE.—The early sorts will now be in flower, and coming into flower. Keep the temperature a few degrees elevated, say at 50° or under, and never much above that—just enough to drive off damp, so that the opening flowers may be kept clear of any damage from condensed moisture, and to ensure a free circulation of pure air; but in no case allow the fire heat to exceed 55°: air must be admitted as soon as the thermometer indicates any rise above that. The plants in tubs and pots may have a little stimulant given them, but not much; half an ounce of guano to one gallon of water will help them to produce fine flowers. The buds on those plants possessing too many of them should be thinned out at once.

THE ROSE HOUSE.—The Roses will be breaking into bud, and will require frequent syringing; fumigating will also be necessary, for the aphides will soon appear. By the middle of the month, more plants may be introduced for succession. Cut back those introduced as soon as they are in the house; give some liquid manure to such as are showing flower, and keep up a heat of 70° or 75°, allowing a fall of 15° or 20° by night. Give no air for the present.

THE LILY-OF-THE-VALLEY PIT.—Keep up a nice mild heat, give air on sunny days, and plenty of water, especially to the Christmas Roses coming into flower, and also to the advancing Lily buds.

THE FERN HOUSE.—Keep up a good heat, with a damp atmosphere, and re-pot small plants. Sow seed and prick off seedlings.

. THE HEATH HOUSE.—Keep the house well ventilated, dry, and at a mild heat. Look out for mildew, and use sulphur to kill it and prevent it; keep the plants temperate at the root, giving no water except sufficient to keep them half dry. Care in watering is now necessary. Cuttings may now be struck.

THE GERANIUM HOUSE.—Keep the house as cool as possible, although a little fire will be necessary, to maintain a healthy atmosphere; keep the plants half dry, with a dry atmosphere. Nip out the points of the leading growth. Those required to flower early, shift into the flowering pots. Admit air daily in mild weather, and turn the plants frequently to induce symmetry of growth; fumigate the house as soon as the least signs of the aphides appear.

THE PINK AND CARNATION HOUSE.—These will now be in full go for flowers, and may be encouraged to mature the late buds by giving the plants some liquid manure. This is a good time to make the full stock of pipings for plants, for forcing next season (see p. 111). Keep up a mild heat, and admit air whenever practicable; but close early.

THE CINERARIA HOUSE.—Keep the house at as low a temperature as possible, but frost-proof; syringe the plants overhead every morning with clean soft water; admit all the air possible every day except when cold, cutting winds prevail, but even then the ground shutters in front may be opened; as soon as the aphides appear fumigate the house in the evening; admit all the air possible to the Calceolarias in the pits;

ward off frost by covering the sashes with dry old hay with straw mats laid on it.

THE GESNERACEOUS HOUSE.—A good lively heat must be kept up for all the classes in this department; the growing plants may be carefully watered, but the dormant ones, such as the Achimenes, Tydæas, Gesneras, &c., must be kept dry; some early Achimenes, Tydæas, and Gloxinias may now be started. (See p. 126.)

THE PEA FRAME.—Sow Early Gem, and give all the air possible to those already advanced in growth.

THE POTATO HOUSE AND FRAMES.—In the beginning of the month plant Myatt's Ash-leaved Kidney, or some other early sort, but I prefer the first; and sow early Radishes on the top.

THE ASPARAGUS PIT.— The beds may now be put to work in earnest; give plenty of water to the roots.

THE EARLY CARROT FRAME.—Sow some Early Horn, or James's Intermediate, and give air to those already up. Protect from frost. (See p. 177.)

### FEBRUARY.

THE EARLY VINERY.—Last month's directions are applicable here in the main. Where the vines have well broke bud, some little disbudding may be necessary; keep up a good heat.

THE LATE VINERY.—The vines are quiet, but the Strawberries may have a little water.

THE PEACH HOUSE.—The Peaches will in some early localities be getting forward in the bud, but should have an abundance of air to keep them back; all pruning both here and on the walls should be done at once.

THE PLUM AND CHERRY HOUSE.—All pruning and training should be finished, and the trees dressed over with a thin solution of Gishurst compound, to destroy the embryo insects.

THE GOOSEBERRY HOUSE. — The trees must now be pruned, thinning them out well, but do not shorten the main leaders much; admit air on mild days.

THE CUCUMBER HOUSE.—Last month's directions are applicable here.

THE MELON HOUSE.—The Melon plants will now be advancing apace; train them out, stop, and encourage them to grow as much as possible. Keep up a heat of 75°, and give an abundance of water. The water should be tepid.

THE PLANT FORCING HOUSE.—Those plants which are coming into flower may have some weak liquid manure once a week. Roses coming into flower must have attention, for the aphides will make their appearance in numbers. Fumigate, or dust them over with tobacco powder; keep up a heat of 75° to 80°. The early training of fast-growing plants, stopping of shrubby ones, and the stimulating of those coming into flower, to obtain finer flowers, are the chief things in hand. The introduction of whatever is desirable for early flowers should be done at once—such as Roses, Hyacinths, Deutzias, Dielytras, Bouvardias, Azaleas, Guelder Roses, Lilacs, Primula cortusoides, Statices, Spiræas, &c. Place the Heliotropes as near the warm end as possible. Sow Rhodanthe, Humea elegans, and Heliotrope seed.

THE CAMELLIA HOUSE.—The plants will now all be coming into flower; give all the air possible and have a mild dry atmosphere in the house, so that the flowers can open freely.

THE ROSE HOUSE.—Last month's routine may be continued. Seed may be sown for new sorts in deep seed-pans; keep the pans in a shady place in this house.

THE LILY-OF-THE-VALLEY AND CHRISTMAS ROSE PIT.—The Christmas Roses will be nearly over where the early sorts are used. Admit all the air possible; the Lilies will now be coming on from thoroughly established plants; give air every mild day by lifting the sashes behind. Give an abundance of water, soaking the bed well, and give some liquid manure to the roots, but do not let it fall on the flowers; these liquid manure waterings will produce extra fine spikes of flower and fine foliage. (See p. 84.)

THE FERNERY.—Continue last month's operations, and shift plants on for large specimens.

THE HEATH HOUSE.—Continue last month's operations, strike cuttings, shift on plants for large specimens, and stop them.

THE GERANIUM HOUSE.—Towards the end of the month shift the whole of the Fancy Pelargoniums from the store pots into the flowering pots, and stop every leading shoot; keep up a good heat for the Tricolors; admit air on every opportunity, i.e. every mild day; give water moderately, and fumigate as soon as the green fly appears.

THE PINK AND CARNATION HOUSE.—See last month's operations, and stop the pipings which are rooted.

THE CINERARIA HOUSE.—Last month's operations may be continued.

THE CALCEOLARIAS.—Herbaceous Calceolarias must be shifted from the small store pots into seven-inch ones. Admit all the air possible every day, and fumigate as soon as the green fly shows itself.

THE POTATO HOUSE AND FRAME.—Those Potatoes that were planted in December will now be up where a fire has been kept going; move the surface a little with a rake.

THE EARLY PEA FRAME AND GLASSES.—The Peas will now be advancing apace; dress them over with the hoe and rake, and admit all the air possible every day.

THE ASPARAGUS PIT.—The Asparagus will now be moving; give an abundance of water and an occasional watering with salt water. Protect from frost by some dry hay or ferns, with a mat on the top.

THE MUSHROOM HOUSE.—The beds made in the autumn will be getting exhausted; make fresh ones, and keep up a mild fire heat.

SEA-KALE.—The Kale will now be in full cut; cut it clean off close to the crown of the old plant, and never let it be above six inches long; then it will be all good and fit for the table. Cut all clean from the pot, and cover it again. Put a stick or long label with the date on it when the Kale was cut, so that you may know for the future. This will save the trouble of searching in vain for the second cut.

RHUBARB FORCING.—The Rhubarb will now be ready. Do the same as for the Sea-kale.

THE CARROT FRAME.—Thin the young Carrots out and sow more. Admit air at all favourable times, and protect from frosts.

*MARCH.*

THE EARLY VINERY.—The bunches will now be formed, and the young wood may be stopped two joints above the bunch. I find that it is not a good practice to stop the young wood (the fruit-bearing laterals) too soon, nor too near the bunch ; one bunch of fruit to a lateral is quite enough. All superfluous wood and spray about the base of the lateral should be taken off. Maintain a heat of 75° to 80°. A moist heat may be encouraged in the house ; no air is necessary.

THE LATE VINERY.—The vines are still quiet, but the eyes are beginning to swell. Water the pot Strawberries well, and keep the house close, notwithstanding the sun heat.

THE PEACH HOUSE.—All pruning must be finished at once. If the Peaches are in pots, water them liberally. Probably the days will be sunny, with sharp frosts at night. Admit air from nine o'clock in the morning till three o'clock in the afternoon on sunny days. Should sharp frosts occur, and the trees be in bloom, some slight protection will be necessary if there are no other means of warding off the effects of the frost upon the blossom. It is a certain and inexpensive method to have a two-inch flow-and-return pipe running close to the front of the house on the ground, heated by a common small saddle boiler. The cost would be very little for a house from forty to sixty feet long, and a little fire put in at five o'clock in the evening would heat it quite enough to ward off the frost for the night. This would be better than screening the trees with gauze or tiffany. Admit no air if the days are cloudy. The Strawberries in pots on the floor should be watered liberally.

THE PLUM HOUSE AND CHERRY HOUSE.—In some localities the Plums and Cherries will be in flower towards the end of this month. Admit air, if possible, on all dry days, so that the pollen may get distributed.

THE GOOSEBERRY HOUSE.—Well syringe the trees in the morning, and give water liberally to those in pots, with now and then some soot in it.

THE CUCUMBER HOUSE.—The house will now be in full bearing. Cut the plants back, thin out the growth, tie in regularly, set the fruit, and water liberally, giving a weekly watering with some liquid manure. Look out sharp for the thrip, and immediately apply the remedy. Strike cuttings for successional plants. Lower the fire heat on sunny mornings, but keep the house close.

THE MELON HOUSE.—Encourage the growth of the plants as much as possible by keeping up a moist and regular heat. Train out the leaders, and stop them once in the course of every two or three feet of growth. Set the fruit every morning. Give top air on very sunny days.

THE PLANT STOVE.—The inmates of this house will now begin to assume a lively aspect, and the exercise of every care and judgment necessary for good success must be exercised. Some plants will require shifting, and some are best not shifted, notwithstanding the roots may fill the pots. Giving weak liquid manure answers the same end as shifting with many things, and is more convenient. When plants must be shifted, and large pots are required, first secure a good drainage by enlarging the aperture at the bottom, and then place an inverted seed-pan over it. Then fill up above the pan with broken pots and some charcoal. Pot off young plants, and sow tender-constituted seed. Keep up a heat of 75° or 80° by day, allowing a fall of 10° by night.

THE CAMELLIA HOUSE.—Last month's observations are applicable here.

THE ROSE HOUSE.—Observe last month's remarks, and keep a sharp eye upon the aphides, using the syringe.

THE LILY-OF-THE-VALLEY PIT.—The Lilies will now be over generally. Give an abundance of water, and admit all the air possible by drawing off the sashes by day, and discontinue the heat. The main thing is now to induce the maturity of the new crowns for flowering for next year.

THE HEATH HOUSE.—Keep the house at a moderate temperature, with plenty of air.

THE GERANIUM HOUSE.—Finish shifting all the plants from the store pots into their flowering pots at once. Stop for the last time all leading growth to induce a dwarf plant, but observe this : the longer the stopping is continued, the later the flowering will be. Water may now be given liberally, with an occasional one of liquid manure of a weak nature. Give an abundance of air, and fumigate as soon as the aphides appear.

THE PINK AND CARNATION HOUSE.—The early flowers will now be over, and the plants may be turned out and thrown away. The young plants, being potted off and stopped, may be removed to a cold frame or pit to harden off, frequently syringing them overhead. Admit all the air possible to the house, and keep the fire on.

THE CINERARIAS.—These will now be in full flower. Discontinue syringing, but fumigate as soon as the green fly appears. Keep a little fire heat, merely as a precaution against cold nights, but no more. Admit all the air possible.

The Calceolarias will require room and air, with frequent fumigations.

THE GESNERACEOUS HOUSE.—The inmates of this department will now begin to assume a beautiful aspect from the development of their foliage; keep up a good lively heat; give water carefully; keep the house close, and shade from too strong a sunlight.

THE POTATO HOUSE, THE PEA FRAMES, THE AS-PARAGUS PIT, THE MUSHROOM HOUSE, SEA-KALE, RHUBARB, CARROT FRAMES, ETC.—May all be referred to last month's remarks.

THE DWARF BEAN HOUSE.—Those coming into bearing must have a good growing heat kept up, with moderate watering. Keep up a moist and humid atmosphere in the house to check the red spider.

*APRIL.*

THE EARLY VINERY.—The Grapes will now be getting a good size, and the last thinning out must be done. Clear off all useless growth, and keep a some-what humid atmosphere in the house, with a good lively heat.

THE LATE VINERY.—The vines will now be break-ing into growth, and must be well looked to, disbud-

P

ding what is not wanted for the fruit or for next year's supply.

THE PEACH HOUSE.—This month is a somewhat important one here. Some of the early trees will be still in progress, and the development of the leaf will be taking place. In these cases some syringing must be done, but not until all the fruit is set; give all the air possible on every sunny day. The greatest importance should be attached to the equal development of the wood-buds in young and progressive trees. The main object is to get as much growth of fruit-bearing wood at the base of the cordon, fan-trained, or even the pyramid, or bush Peach, as there is at the extremities. The aphides will soon be troublesome, and the syringe must be well applied to those trees that have set fruit. The Strawberries on the floor must be well watered.

THE PLUM HOUSE AND THE CHERRY HOUSE.— Admit all the air possible till the fruit is set; then syringe freely every day.

THE GOOSEBERRY HOUSE.—Continue last month's work.

THE CUCUMBER HOUSE.—Discontinue the fire heat all day, and merely light a fire in the evening that will last till the morning; keep the house closed.

THE MELON HOUSE.—Observe the remarks made last month. Look out for the thrip, and apply tobacco powder with a dredging box.

THE CAMELLIA HOUSE.—Most of the flowers will now be over, or by the end of the month. Encourage the plants to make new growth as much as possible by keeping the house closed, syringing overhead, and having a little fire heat for a fortnight.

THE ROSE HOUSE.—Last month's remarks are applicable here.

THE GERANIUM HOUSE.—Last month's remarks generally are applicable here.

THE PINK AND CARNATION HOUSE.—By the end of the month these will be over, and may be cleared out; and the room occupied with herbaceous Calceolarias.

THE CINERARIA HOUSE.—By the end of the month these will have done flowering, and may then be removed to a cold frame if seed is desired, and the plants are choice sorts from which offsets are wanted. The house may then be filled with Calceolarias.

## MAY.

THE EARLY VINERY.—The Grapes will now be changing colour, and must have air night and day if a good colour is wanted. Keep the shutters open night and day in front of the house, close to the ground; and the ventilators at the top also, having an equal and mild heat at the same time.

THE LATE VINERY.—Last month's remarks are applicable here. The Strawberry pots on the floor or otherwise will have done fruiting, and should be turned out and planted in the ground, where they will bear fruit for years to come.

THE PEACH HOUSE.—Last month's remarks are applicable here. Daily syringing with clean soft water and proper ventilation are the chief things to be done; with a timely thinning out of the fruit, allowing one fruit (Peach or Nectarine) to a square foot, for extra fine fruit. The same thing applies to the cordon Peaches behind the screens on the wall.

The Plum House and Cherry House.—Admit air freely, and syringe daily.

The Gooseberry House.—Syringe copiously every day.

The Cucumber House.—Make fresh beds, and put in strong young plants for summer work.  No fire heat is required for the summer.  Ventilate at the top on hot days, but cold draughts must be avoided.  Shut up early and syringe to keep up a humid atmosphere.

The Melon House.—Observe last month's remarks, and when the fruit is ripening be less liberal with the water.

The Plant Stove.—This month is an active time for the growing of all plants and the development of fine specimens.  Due attention to early potting, training, stopping of the leaders, the creation of vapour, checking of the insect tribes, &c., are the chief things to attend to.

The Camellia House.—By the end of the month —some before, and some a little later—the plants will have made the terminal bud ; then admit all the air possible, and keep the house open night and day.

The Rose House.—Turn all the plants out by the end of the month ; and cut them back, re-pot, and plunge them in some old tan, coal ashes, or sawdust on a south border, and encourage them to make strong wood.

The Balsam House.—Admit all the air possible ; give an abundance of water, and get all the light among the plants that is possible.

The Asparagus Pit.—Discontinue heat, and remove the sashes entirely.

The other departments, as regards vegetables, may

by the end of the month be treated as for out-door crops, except the Dwarf Kidney Beans, which must still be protected.

## *JUNE.*

THE EARLY VINERY.—Last month's remarks are applicable here.

THE PEACH HOUSE.—Last month's remarks are the same for this month.

THE PLUM AND CHERRY HOUSES.—Admit all the air possible daily, and syringe freely.

THE CUCUMBER HOUSE.—Last month's remarks are applicable here.

The same may be said of the other departments.

## *JULY.*

THE LATE VINERY.—The Grapes will now be filling up, and should be tied out a little at the shoulders of the bunches. Keep the house close until the berries begin to change colour, except on very hot days and the squares are large; then top ventilation should be given from ten o'clock in the morning till three in the afternoon, when the house should be closed, and the floor watered, to keep up a certain amount of humidity, to help the development of the berries and to keep down the red spider.

THE PEACH HOUSE AND WALL PEACHES.—Now is the critical time in the management of these, to insure success ultimately. If the house and wall screens are not kept open constantly night and day, the trees may be suffocated, the red spider engendered, and the final end of the trees not far off. Keep the syringe going daily;

pinch in the laterals, and regulate the laterals on cordons to one leader right and left, and thin out the fruit.

THE CHERRY HOUSE.—The syringing may be less than before, but it can never be wholly dispensed with on account of aphides.

THE PLUM HOUSE.—Continue syringing, and admit all the air possible night and day. Nip in all the laterals as they make two or three inches of wood.

THE CUCUMBER AND MELON HOUSES.—Observe last month's remarks.

THE PLANT STOVE.—Everything will be in full growth and have a gay appearance; the chief business here will be to obtain healthy and handsome plants by regulating all the leading growth, getting as much light as possible on all sides of the plants, and the ripening off of some of the early flowering kinds.

THE GERANIUM HOUSE.—Cut down all very early flowering plants; strike the short cuttings, and pot the earlier struck cuttings intended for large and early plants.

THE BALSAM HOUSE.—Admit all the air possible; give an abundance of water, and set the plants so far apart that the light can get at them all round, and when they are well formed give them some weak liquid manure.

THE CUCUMBER HOUSE.—No fire heat will be required from May till September.


*AUGUST.*

THE LATE VINERY.—The Grapes will now require an abundance of air day and night, on all sides, if good-coloured fruit is wanted. Do not shut the house at all, let the weather be what it may ; but if several days together continue cold, wet, and dull, light a fire to raise the heat a little, but on no account close the house. Keep the young wood thin.

THE PEACH HOUSE AND WALL-SCREEN PEACHES.— Last month's remarks are applicable here as a rule ; but discontinue the syringing, if the fruit is ripening. A sharp eye must be kept upon the red spider ; and some sulphur should be kept placed on several money slates, so that the sun can play full upon them ; this will give off fumes sufficient to keep the spider in check (see last month).

As regards all the other departments, last month's directions may be referred to.

### SEPTEMBER.

THE EARLY AND LATE VINERIES.—The chief thing now is to ripen the young wood thoroughly and to bring the growth to a standstill. To promote this withhold all stimulants, and place the sashes on the frames, so as to prevent the rains falling on the border. Admit all the air possible to the branches, so that the ripening of the wood can be perfected by the influence of the atmosphere.

THE PEACH HOUSE.—Daily watering of Peaches in pots (but no syringing) must be done, if the fruit is ripening. The cordon Peaches should be regulated in the new wood by pinching in the laterals, but the young wood right and left for next year's fruiting must not be pinched in, only the sub-laterals and all such growth as is not required for fruiting.

THE CHERRY HOUSE.—The Cherry is so liable to the aphides pest that to cease syringing is to give license for its attacks; syringing, therefore, must be continued as much as possible, and all the air admitted that it is practicable to get.

THE PLUM HOUSE.—Similar treatment to that of the Cherry in the house, is necessary. Pinching in of the laterals, and an abundance of air night and day constantly, are essential to ensure success.

THE CUCUMBER HOUSE.—Make good and substantial fresh beds, in readiness for planting strong plants, early next month, for winter work.

THE PLANT STOVE.—The chief thing now is to ripen the young growth made through the summer months, by keeping up a moderate fire heat and by discontinuing to a great extent the amount of watering to those plants that have done flowering and show signs of rest.

THE GESNERACEOUS HOUSE.—Some of the inmates of this department will be showing signs of rest; less watering must therefore be given to those which have done flowering, but not so as to immediately dry them off; give enough to mature the new parts.

THE MUSHROOM HOUSE.—Preparation must now be made for making good beds for the winter. (See p. 181.)

## OCTOBER.

THE PEACH HOUSE AND PEACH WALL.—By the middle of the month cordon Peaches should be lifted; i.e. dig round each tree and free the roots, lift the tree, and replant it just where it was. This checks the rank growth and keeps them tame. Do not be afraid to do it, for they will be none the worse for the move. This applies to all Peach and Plum trees that are young and have a tendency to make too much wood. The trees in the house must be watered after the replanting. Towards the end of the month new plantations may be made. Keep the ventilators open.

THE PLUM AND CHERRY HOUSE.—Last month's remarks are applicable here.

THE CAMELLIA HOUSE.—Towards the end of the month the sashes may be drawn up at night, but admit all the air possible by day. Those in pots out of doors may be brought in.

THE GERANIUM HOUSE.—Towards the middle of the month the old plants may be shaken out of the pots they have flowered in, and the ball reduced, and then repotted into small pots, five-inch or six-inch, according to the size of the plants, and then housed for the winter. Give water very moderately, and all the air possible daily.

THE CINERARIA HOUSE.—About the middle of the month—sooner or a little later, according to the state of the weather, being careful of frost—clean over the pots of young Cinerarias, and house them, admitting air and syringing daily. Seedling Calceolarias should be placed in the pit.

THE PLANT STOVE.—Now is the time to see that all plants intended for forcing are thoroughly established in the pots, and the wood well ripened. Keep up a day temperature of 60° to 70°, and some plants may now be introduced for early flowering.

THE PINK AND CARNATION HOUSE.—In the beginning of the month house the plants for forcing. (See p. 111.)

## NOVEMBER.

THE EARLY VINERY.—The vines may now be all finally pruned, dressed over with soot and sulphur and soft soap, or a thick solution of Gishurst compound, and tied up ready for work.

THE LATE VINERY.—Early in the month new vines may be planted. Prune those that are established, and top-dress the roots of all of them with any manure but stable manure, which should be studiously avoided (see p. 22).

THE PEACH HOUSE.—Moderate watering, but not too much. If the plants have a tendency to grow freely, keep them rather short of water, so as to bring them to a state of rest. Open the ventilators every day, and if the plants are less vigorous than they should be, top-dress the borders with some mild manure.

THE PLUM AND CHERRY HOUSES.—Similar treatment to that recommended for the Peach is applicable here.

THE GOOSEBERRY HOUSE.—Towards the end of the month prune the trees and well manure the ground, and fork it over a few inches, but never dig immediately on the roots near the stem.

THE CUCUMBER HOUSE.—Keep up a good brisk heat of 70° or 75° with a decrease of 10° by night; keep the house close, and fumigate on the least appearance of the thrip, or dust the vines with tobacco powder; set the fruit daily.

THE ROSE HOUSE.—Introduce the plants and prune them; keep up a moderate heat at first.

THE LILY-OF-THE-VALLEY AND CHRISTMAS ROSE PIT.

—By the middle of the month clean over the surface of both, and top-dress the Hellebores with a good dressing of decayed stable manure made fine. Sow the lilies with an inch of fine decomposed stable manure or leaf mould, and sand over the surface; put on a slow fire and place on the sashes. Make new plantations.

THE PINK AND CARNATION HOUSE.—Keep up a good heat, and syringe the plants.

THE CINERARIA HOUSE.—Admit all the air possible and syringe every morning with clean soft water, and should the aphides persist in troubling the plants, smoke them in the morning.

THE GERANIUM HOUSE.—Admit as much air as possible, and give no more water than is absolutely necessary to prevent the plants from flagging, keeping them merely moving.

THE EARLY PEA-FRAME.—Sow some ' Little Gem ' during the month.

THE ASPARAGUS PIT.—Top-dress the bed and put on the sashes.

Sea-kale and Rhubarb may now be covered up for forcing (see pp. 172 ; 175).


*DECEMBER.*

THE EARLY VINERY.—The remarks for January are applicable in this department and also in the Late Vinery.

THE PEACH HOUSE AND WALL-SCREEN PEACHES.— The remarks for January are applicable here also.

THE PLUM AND CHERRY HOUSE.—The remarks for January are applicable here also.

The same may be said of the Gooseberry house.

THE CUCUMBER HOUSE.—The remarks for January should be observed during this month likewise.

THE MELON HOUSE.—The remarks for January are the same here.

THE PLANT HOUSE, OR STOVE.—The remarks for January are applicable here also.

THE CAMELLIA HOUSE.—The remarks for January are practicable here also.

THE ROSE HOUSE.—I cannot do better than refer the reader to the month of January for the work now to be done here.

THE LILY-OF-THE-VALLEY AND CHRISTMAS ROSE PIT.—The observations for January are good here also.

THE HEATH HOUSE.—The remarks made in January are practicable here also.

THE GERANIUM HOUSE.—The same remarks made in January are good now.

THE PINK AND CARNATION HOUSE.—The remarks for January are practicable here also.

THE CINERARIA HOUSE.—Observe the remarks made for January for this department.

THE GESNERACEOUS HOUSE.—The same remarks for January are practicable here.

THE EARLY POTATO FRAME.—In the middle of the month plant some early sorts, such as ' Myatt's Ash-leaved Kidney,' ' Early Frame,' or any preferable kinds, but do not be misled by bombast. I find there are no earlier or better sorts than those named, but both require plenty of decayed or half-decayed leaf-mould to grow them in.

THE EARLY PEA FRAME.—Manure the bed moderately and sow ' Little Gem.'

THE ASPARAGUS PIT.—See the remarks for January.

THE EARLY CARROT FRAME.—The remarks for January are practicable here.

THE FORCING OF RHUBARB AND SEA-KALE.—The remarks for these, and upon the Mushroom house, are the same as for November.

# INDEX.

PRINTED BY
SPOTTISWOODE AND CO., NEW-STREET SQUARE
LONDON

# BY THE SAME AUTHOR↑

## *A PLAIN GUIDE TO GOOD GARDENING;* or, How to Grow

Vegetables, Fruits, and Flowers. With Practical Notes on Soils, Manures, Seeds, Planting, Laying-out of Gardens and Grounds, &c. By S. WOOD. Fourth Edition, with considerable Additions, &c., and numerous Illustrations. Crown 8vo. 3*s*. 6*d*. cloth.

'May be recommended to young gardeners, cottagers, and specially to amateurs, for the plain, simple, and trustworthy information it gives on common matters too often neglected.'
GARDENERS' CHRONICLE.

'A thoroughly useful guide-book for the amateur gardener.'—DAILY TELEGRAPH.

'A very good book, and one to be highly recommended as a practical guide. The practical directions are excellent.'—ATHENÆUM.

'We may safely commend Mr. Wood's book to all those who aspire to really good gardening, being satisfied that its principles are sound and its directions practical, and that those who take it for their manual will be in no danger whatever of being led astray.'
SPECTATOR.

'Written by a practical man, and gives practical instructions which it is easy for amateurs to understand.'—SATURDAY REVIEW.

## *MULTUM-IN-PARVO GARDENING;* or, How to make One

Acre of Land produce £620 a year, by the Cultivation of Fruits and Vegetables ; also, How to Grow Flowers in Three Glass Houses, so as to realise £176 per annum clear Profit. By SAMUEL WOOD. Fifth Edition, revised. Crown 8vo. 1*s*. sewed.

'We recommend this book, which is suited to the case of the amateur and gentleman's gardener, as well as to the market grower, who cannot fail to share the benefits to be derived by a careful study of Mr. Wood's routine.'—GARDENERS' MAGAZINE.

'Gives the fullest directions how to cultivate fruit and vegetables with the minimum of glass and the maximum of profit.'—TRUTH.

'Of all the practical guides to the amateur, as well as being valuable to non-gardeners, Mr. Wood's book is the most accurate and concise. Every subject treated on is written in the plainest and most unmistakable language.'—HORTICULTURAL RECORD.

'The book is well worth a careful study ; the calculations as to outlay and profit are fairly put, and with a favourable climate we think would be realised.'—SCOTSMAN.

'Should be read by all who contemplate growing for market and profit.'—FARMER.

'All who possess a garden should procure Mr. Wood's cheap volume.'—ONCE A WEEK.

## *THE LADIES' MULTUM-IN-PARVO FLOWER GARDEN* and

AMATEURS' COMPLETE GUIDE. By SAMUEL WOOD, Author of 'Good Gardening' &c. With numerous Illustrations. Crown 8vo. 3*s*. 6*d*. cloth.

'Sound but simple instructions, likely to be useful to lady gardeners.'—FLORIST.

'The author is a practical man. We recommend the book to any one desirous of becoming a "gardener" in the popular acceptation of the term.'—ENGLISH MECHANIC.

'A very large amount of information. The book is full of sound advice.'
DAILY CHRONICLE.

'Full of shrewd hints and useful instructions, based on a lifetime of experience.'
SCOTSMAN.

'Written in an unpretending style by a practical man.'—BRISTOL MERCURY.

'Amateurs should, with the assistance of such a guide, and the immense facilities which are now within their reach, find it easy to gratify their taste for gardening.'
NEWCASTLE COURANT.

CROSBY LOCKWOOD & SON, 7 Stationers' Hall Court, London, E.C.

A SHORT-TITLE LIST OF

# SCIENTIFIC, TECHNICAL

# AND INDUSTRIAL BOOKS

PUBLISHED BY

## CROSBY LOCKWOOD & SON

(C. M. LOCKWOOD)

### 7 STATIONERS' HALL COURT, LONDON, E.C.4

*Telegrams*  
CROSBY LOCKWOOD, CENT. LONDON

*Telephone*  
4421 CENTRAL

*POST FREE ON APPLICATION*

COMPLETE DETAILED CATALOGUE

PUBLICATIONS OF THE BRITISH ENGINEERING
STANDARDS ASSOCIATION

AND

THE AMERICAN CHEMICAL CATALOGUE CO.

NOTE.—*The prices herein quoted are subject to revision
without notice*

JANUARY 1925

A SHORT-TITLE LIST OF

# SCIENTIFIC, TECHNICAL AND INDUSTRIAL BOOKS

PUBLISHED BY

# CROSBY LOCKWOOD & SON

*All Published Prices are net.*

*All Published Prices are net.*

Chemistry—Industrial and Manufacturing Chemistry : Part II.—
   Inorganic. Martin. Royal 8vo. In 2 Volumes. Per vol.  . 28s
Civil Engineering Design. Barber. Demy 8vo .  .  .  .  7s 6d
Civil Engineering Geology. Fox. Royal 8vo  .  .  .  . 18s
Clerk of Works. Metson. Crown 8vo .  .  .  .  .  3s 6d
Clockmaking : Past and Present. Gordon. Demy 8vo  . *Nearly Ready*
Clock Repairing and Making. Garrard. Crown 8vo .  .  .  6s
Coal and Iron Industries of the United Kingdom. Meade. 8vo £1 8s
Coal Mining. Glover. Crown 8vo .  .  .  .  .  .  2s
Coal Mining, Practical. Cockin. Crown 8vo  .  .  .  6s
Coal Mining Notes and Formulæ for Students. Merivale. Small
   Crown 8vo .  .  .  .  .  .  .  .  .  3s 6d
Cocoanut Cultivation. Coghlan and Hinchley. Sm. Crown 8vo  .  4s
Coking Practice. Byrom and Christopher—
   Volume I. Raw Materials and Coke. Demy 8vo  .  . 10s 6d
   Volume II. By-Products. Demy 8vo  .  .  .  . 10s 6d
Colliery Working and Management. Bulman and Redmayne.
   Medium 8vo .  .  .  .  .  .  *New Ed. Preparing*
Colorimetric Analysis. Snell. Demy 8vo  .  .  .  . 10s 6d
Combustion in the Gas Producer. Korevaar. Demy 8vo  ·  . 15s
Commerce, Lessons in. Gambaro. Crown 8vo .  .  .  .  5s
Commercial Correspondent, Foreign. Baker. Crown 8vo .  .  7s 6d
Compressed Air Work and Diving. Boycott. Medium 8vo  . 10s 6d
Concrete : its Nature and Uses. Sutcliffe. Crown 8vo  .  . 10s 6d
Concrete for House, Farm, and Estate. Ballard. Demy 8vo .  3s 6d
Confectioner, Modern Flour. Wells. Crown 8vo  .  .  .  2s
Confectionery, Ornamental. Wells. Crown 8vo .  .  .  7s 6d
Continuous Railway Brakes. Reynolds. 8vo  .  .  .  .  9s
Controllers for Electric Motors. James. Demy 8vo .  .  . 21s
Cotton Industry. Crabtree. Crown 8vo .  .  .  .  .  6s
Creation, The Twin Records of. Le Vaux. 8vo .  .  .  .  5s
Curves, Tables of Tangential Angles and Multiples. Beazeley .  .  5s
Dairying (British and Colonial). Sutherland Thomson. Demy 8vo  9s
Dairying Industry. Sutherland Thomson. Demy 8vo  .  . 10s 6d
Damp Walls. Blake. Crown 8vo .  .  .  .  .  .  8s 6d
Dangerous Goods. Aeby. Royal 8vo .  .  .  .  .  . 30s
Dangerous Goods. Phillips. Crown 8vo  .  .  .  . 10s 6d
Decorator's Assistant. Small Crown 8vo  .  .  .  .  2s 6d
Deep-Level Mines of the Rand. Denny. Royal 8vo .  .  . 25s
Dentistry (Mechanical). Hunter. Crown 8vo  .  .  .  .  6s
Diesel Engine. Wells & Wallis-Tayler. Demy 8vo  .  .  . 15s
Dog Book (Complete). Bruette: Large Crown 8vo .  .  . 16s
Dredges and Dredging. Prelini. Royal 8vo  .  .  .  . 21s
Drilling for Gold and Other Minerals. Denny. Medium 8vo . 12s 6d
Dynamo (How to Make). Crofts. Crown 8vo .  .  .  2s 6d
Dynamo Electric Machinery. Hausmann. Demy 8vo  .  . 21s
Dynamos (Alternating and Direct Current). Sewell. Lge. Cr. 8vo 7s 6d
Dynamos (Management of). Lummis-Paterson. Crown 8vo  .  .  6s

*All Published Prices are net.*

Earthenware, The Manufacture of. Sandeman. Crown 8vo  .  . 12s
Earthwork Diagrams. Erskine-Murray and Kirton. 5s ; mounted, 7s 6d
Earthwork Manual. Graham. 18mo  .  .  .  .  .  . 3s 6d
Earthwork Tables. Broadbent and Campin. Crown 8vo .  .  . 6s
Earthwork Tables. Buck. On a sheet .  .  .  .  .  . 3s 6d
Electric Light. Urquhart. Crown 8vo .  .  .  .  .  . 7s 6d
Electric Light Fitting. Urquhart. Crown 8vo  .  .  .  .  . 5s
Electric Light for Country Houses. Knight. Crown 8vo .  . 1s 6d
Electric Lighting and Starting for Motor Cars. Cross. Demy 8vo 28s
Electric Lighting and Heating. Walker. Fcap. 8vo .  .  .  . 5s
Electric Motors. Crocker and Arendt. Medium 8vo .  .  . 18s
Electric Power Conductors. Del Marr. Large Crown 8vo.  . 12s 6d
Electric Power Conductors. Perrine. Medium 8vo.  .  .  . 21s
Electric Power Stations. Klingenberg. Crown 4to  .  .  .  . 28s
Electric Power Station : A 130,000-Kilowatt Power Station. Klingen-
     berg. Crown 4to.  .  .  .  .  .  .  .  .  .  . 21s
Electric Spark Ignition in Internal Combustion Engines. Morgan.
     Medium 8vo .  .  .  .  .  .  .  .  .  .  . 6s
Electric Traction and Transmission Engineering. Sheldon and
     Hausmann. Large Crown 8vo .  .  .  .  .  .  . 21s
Electric Wiring Diagrams and Switchboards. Harrison. Crown 8vo 12s 6d
Electrical Circuits and Connections. Bowker. Medium 8vo.  . 15s
Electrical Dictionary. Sloane. Large Crown 8vo  .  .  .  . 21s
Electrical Engineering (Elementary). Alexander. Crown 8vo .  . 5s
Electrical Engineering. Sewell. Large Crown 8vo  .  .  . 7s 6d
Electrical Horology. Langman and Ball. Crown 8vo  .  . 7s 6d
Electrical Installation Work. Havelock. Demy 8vo .  .  . 15s
Electrical Transmission of Energy. Abbott. Royal 8vo .  .  . 30s
Electrical Transmission of Energy—Three-Phase Transmission.
     Brew. Demy 8vo  .  .  .  .  .  .  *New Ed. Preparing*
Electricity as Applied to Mining. Lupton. Medium 8vo .  . 12s 6d
Electricity in Factories and Workshops. Haslam. Large Cr. 8vo . 8s 6d
Electro-Plating. Urquhart. Crown 8vo.  .  .  .  .  . 7s 6d
Electro-Plating. Watt. Crown 8vo  .  .  .  .  .  . 5s
Electro-Plating and Electro-Refining of Metals. Watt and Philip.
     Large Crown 8vo.  .  .  .  .  .  .  .  .  . 15s
Embroiderer's Book of Design. Delamotte. Oblong 8vo .  .  . 3s
Engineering Drawing. Maxton and Malden. Crown 8vo .  . 8s 6d
Engineering Progress (1863-6). Humber. Imperial 4to, half
     morocco  .  .  .  . Price £12 12s ; each volume, £3 3s
Engineering Workshop Handbook. Pull. Royal 16mo  . 3s 6d
Engineering Workshop Notes and Data. Pull. Pott 16mo  . 2s 6d
Engineer's Handbook (Practical). Hutton. Medium 8vo .  .  . 21s
Engineer's Measuring Tools. Pull. Crown 8vo .  .  .  . 4s 6d
Engineer's and Millwright's Assistant. Templeton. 18mo  .  . 3s
Engineer's Year-Book. Kempe. Crown 8vo  .  . *Annually* 30s
Engineering Standards Association's Reports and Specifications.
                                 *Separate List on Application*
Entropy as a Tangible Conception. Wheeler. Demy 8vo  . 8s 6d

*All Published Prices are net.*

Excavation (Earth and Rock). Prelini. Royal 8vo . . . . 21s
Explosives—High Explosives. Colver. Royal 8vo . . . £3 3s
Explosives—Nitro-Explosives. Sanford. Demy 8vo . . . . 12s
Factory Accounts. Garcké and Fells. Demy 8vo . . . . 15s
Farm Account Book. Woodman. Folio . . . . . 10s 6d
Farm Gas Engines. Brate. Crown 8vo. . . . . 6s 6d
Farmers' Tables and Memoranda. Francis. Waistcoat-pocket size 2s 6d
Farmers' Labour and Account Book. Dalley. Fcap. Folio . . 6s
Farming, Practical. Shepherd. Demy 8vo . . . . . 5s
Fertilizing Materials, Mining and Manufacture. Lloyd. Crown 8vo . 12s
Fire Protection in Buildings. Holt. Demy 8vo . . . . . 9s
Forcing Garden. Wood. Crown 8vo . . . . . . 4s
Foreshores. Latham. Crown 8vo . . . . . . 2s 6d
Forestry, Practical. Curtis. Crown 8vo . . . . . . 6s
Forestry : Complete Yield Tables for. Maw. Oblong . . 7s 6d
French Conversation, Guide to. De Fivas. 32mo . . . 2s 6d
French Grammar : De Fivas' New Grammar of French
    Grammars . . . . . . . . . . . 2s 6d
    Key to the Above . . . . . . . . . 3s 6d
French for Beginners. De Fivas. Sm. Crown 8vo . . . 1s 6d
French Language : Introduction. De Fivas. Crown 8vo . . 2s 6d
French Polishing. Bitmead. Crown 8vo. . . . . . 2s 6d
Fretcutting, The Art of Modern. Makinson. Crown 8vo . . 2s 6d
Founders' Manual. Payne. Crown 8vo. . . . . . 24s
Fruit Growing. Douglass. Large Crown 8vo . . . . 7s 6d
Gas Engine Handbook. Roberts. Crown 8vo . . . . 12s 6d
Gas Engineers' Pocket-Book. O'Connor. Crown 8vo *New Ed. Preparing*
Gas Manufacture, Chemistry of. Royle. Demy 8vo . . . 16s
Gas Meters. Gilbert. Crown 8vo . . . . . . . 7s 6d
Gas and Oil Engine Management. Bale. Crown 8vo . . 3s 6d
Gasfitting and Appliances. Briggs and Henwood. Crown 8vo . 6s
Geometry of Compasses. Byrne. Crown 8vo . . . . 3s 6d
Geometry for Technical Students. Sprague. Crown 8vo . . 2s
Gold Extraction, Cyanide Process of. Eissler. 8vo . . . 8s 6d
Gold, Metallurgy of. Eissler. Medium 8vo . . . . . 25s
Gold Mining Machinery. Tinney. Medium 8vo . . . . 12s 6d
Gold Working : Jeweller's Assistant. Gee. Crown 8vo . . 8s 6d
Goldsmith's Handbook. Gee. Crown 8vo . . . . . 6s
Granites and our Granite Industries. Harris. Crown 8vo. . . 3s
Grazing. The Complete Grazier, and Farmer's and Cattle Breeder's
    Assistant. Youatt, Fream and Bear. Royal 8vo . . . 36s
Hand Sketching for Mining Students. Lodge and Harwood.
    Oblong Demy 4to . . . . . . . . . . 5s
Handrailing and Staircasing. Collings. Crown 8vo . . . 3s 6d
Handybooks for Handicrafts. Hasluck. Crown 8vo.
    Metal Turner's Handybook . . . . . . . 1s 6d
    Wood Turner's Handybook. . . . . . . . 1s 6d
    Watch Jobber's Handybook . . . . . . . 1s 6d

*All Published Prices are net.*

Handybooks for Handicrafts—(*contd.*)
Pattern Maker's Handybook . . . . . . . 1s 6d
Mechanic's Workshop Handybook . . . . . . 1s 6d
Model Engineer's Handybook . . . . . . . 1s 6d
Clock Jobber's Handybook . . . . . . . . 1s 6d
Cabinet Worker's Handybook . . . . . . . 1s 6d
Woodworker's Handybook . . . . . . . . 1s 6d
Heat, Expansion of Structures by. Keily. Crown 8vo . . . 4s
Hoisting Machinery. Horner. Crown 8vo . . . . . 8s 6d
Horticultural Note-Book. Newsham. Fcap. 8vo . . . . 7s 6d
Hot Water and Steam Heating and Ventilation. King. Med. 8vo . 21s
House Owner's Estimator. Simon. Crown 8vo . . . . . 4s
House Painting. Davidson. Crown 8vo . . . . . 7s 6d
House Planning—How to Plan a House. Samson. Crown 8vo . 6s
House Property. Tarbuck. 12mo . . . . . . . 7s 6d
Houses for the Community. James and Yerbury. Royal 4to. 31s 6d
Houses, Villas, Cottages, and Bungalows for Britishers and Americans
      Abroad. Samson. Demy 8vo . . . . . . 7s 6d
Illuminating and Missal Painting. Whithard. Crown 8vo . . 6s
Illumination, Art of. Delamotte. Small 4to . . . . 7s 6d
Inflammable Gas and Vapour in the Air. Clowes. Crown 8vo . 6s
Interest Calculator. Campbell. Crown 8vo . . . . . . 3s
Internal Combustion Engines. Carpenter. Medium 8vo . . . 30s
Internal Combustion Engines. Institute of Marine Engineers.
      Demy 8vo . . . . . . . . . . 12s 6d
Inwood's Tables of Interest and Mortality. Schooling. Medium 8vo 21s
Iron and Metal Trades Companion. Downie . . . . . 9s
Iron Ores of Great Britain and Ireland. Kendall. Crown 8vo . 18s
Iron-Plate Weight Tables. Burlinson and Simpson. 4to . . . 25s
Irrigation (Pioneer). Mawson. Demy 8vo . . . . 12s 6d
Jigs, Tools and Fixtures (Drawing and Design). Gates. Crown 8vo. 8s 6d
Journalism. Mackie. Crown 8vo . . . . . . 2s 6d
Labour Disputes, Conciliation and Arbitration in. Jeans. Crown 8vo 2s 6d
Land Ready Reckoner. Arman. Crown 8vo . . . . . 4s
Land Valuer's Assistant. Hudson. Royal 32mo . . . 4s 6d
Lathe Design, Construction, and Operation. Perrigo. Med. 8vo . 18s
Lathe Work. Hasluck. Crown 8vo . . . . . . 6s
Law : Every Man's Own Lawyer. A Barrister. Large Crown 8vo 15s
Laxton's and Lockwood's Builder's Price Book. Crown 8vo *Annually* 7s 6d
Lead, Metallurgy of. Eissler. Crown 8vo . . . . . 15s
Leather Chemistry. Harvey. Demy 8vo . . . . . 15s
Leather Manufacture. Watt. 8vo . . . . . . 15s
Letter Painting. Badenock and Prior. Crown 8vo . . . 2s
Light and Colour in Advertising and Merchandising. Luckiesh.
      Demy 8vo . . . . . . . . . . 16s
Light and Work. Luckiesh. Demy 8vo . . . . . 21s
Lightning Conductors, Modern. Hedges. Medium 8vo . . . 8s
Limes and Cements. Dancaster. Large Crown 8vo . . . 7s 6d

*All Published Prices are net.*

Liquid Fuels for Internal Combustion Engines. Moore. Demy 8vo 15s
Locomotive Engine. Weatherburn. Crown 8vo . . . . 3s 6d
Locomotive Engine Development. Stretton. Crown 8vo . . . 5s
Machine Shop Tools. Van Dervoort. Medium 8vo . . . . 25s
Magnetos for Automobilists. Bottone. Crown 8vo . . . 2s 6d
Marble and Marble Working. Renwick. Medium 8vo . . . 16s
Marble Decoration. Blagrove. Crown 8vo . . . . . 3s 6d
Marine Diesel Oil Engines. Sothern. Medium 8vo . . . . 21s
Marine Engineer's Pocket-Book. Wannan. 18mo . . . 7s 6d
Marine Engine Indicator Cards. Sothern. Medium 8vo . . . 15s
Marine Engineers' "Verbal" Notes and Sketches. Sothern:
    Medium 8vo . . . . . . . . . . 40s
Marine Engineering. Wheeler. Royal 8vo. In 2 volumes,
    Vol 1 . . . . . . . . . . . 18s
Marine Engines and Boilers. Bauer. Medium 8vo . . . . 25s
Marine Gas Engines. Clark. Crown 8vo . . . . . 10s 6d
Marine Steam Turbine. Sothern. Medium 8vo . . . . 40s
Marine Steam Turbines. Bauer. Medium 8vo . . . . 12s 6d
Marine Works. Latham. Demy 8vo . . . . . . 16s
Masonry. Purchase. Royal 8vo . . . . . . . 9s
Masonry Dams from Inception to Completion. Courtney. 8vo 10s 6d
Measures (British and American). Foley. Folio . . . 8s 6d
Mechanical Engineering Terms (Lockwood's Dictionary of).
    Horner. Crown 8vo . . . . . . . . 9s
Mechanical Handling and Storing of Material. Zimmer. Royal 8vo 63s
Mechanics Condensed. Hughes. Crown 8vo . . . . 2s 6d
Mechanics of Air Machinery. Weisbach. Royal 8vo . . . 25s
Mechanics' Workshop Companion. Templeton & Hutton. Fcp. 8vo 7s 6d
Mercantile Calculation Tables. Kirchner. Demy 4to. . . £3 3s
Metal Plate Work (Principles and Processes). Barrett. Crown 8vo 3s 6d
Metal-Turning. Horner. Large Crown 8vo . . . . 12s 6d
Metallurgical Analysis (Technical Methods of). Scott. Royal 8vo 42s
Metals and their Alloys. Brannt and Vickers. Royal 8vo . . £2 10s
Metrology. Jackson. Large Crown 8vo . . . . . 12s 6d
Military Observation Balloons. Widmer. Crown 8vo . . . 16s
Milling Machines. Horner. Medium 8vo . . . . . 15s
Mine Drainage. Michell. Royal 8vo . . . . . . 25s
Mine Rescue Work and Organization. Bulman and Mills.
    Demy 8vo . . . . . . . . . . 12s
Mine Wagon and its Lubrication. Pamely. Medium 8vo . . 7s 6d
Minerals and Mining (Earthy). Davies. Crown 8vo . . . 12s 6d
Minerals and Mining (Metalliferous). Davies. Large Crown 8vo 12s 6d
Miners and Metallurgists, Pocket-Book for. Power. Fcap. 8vo . 7s 6d
Mining, British. Hunt. Super Royal 8vo . . . . . 42s
Mining Calculations. O'Donahue. Crown 8vo . . . . 3s 6d
Mining Examination Questions (1,200). Kerr. Demy 8vo . 2s 6d
Mining, Physics and Chemistry of. Byrom. Crown 8vo . . . 6s
Mining : Machinery for Metalliferous Mines. Davies. Medium 8vo 25s

*All Published Prices are net.*

Motor Bodywork. Butler Crown 4to . . . . . £2 12s 6d
Motor Car and Coach Painting. Oliver. Crown 4to . . . 28s 6d
Motor Car Catechism. Knight. Crown 8vo . . . . . 3s 6d
Motor Car Construction. Brewer. Demy 8vo . . . . . 9s
Motor Car Mechanism and Management. Shepherd. Crown 8vo 4s 6d
Motor Cycle Overhauling. Shepherd. Crown 8vo . . . 2s 6d
Motor Lorry Design Construction. Schaefer. Medium 8vo . . 18s
Motor Tyres. Ferguson. Crown 8vo . . . . . . 3s 6d
Motor Vehicles. Fraser and Jones. Medium 8vo . . . . 16s
Naval Architect's and Shipbuilder's Pocket-Book. Mackrow and
    Woollard. Fcap. 8vo . . . . . . . . . 16s
Oil-Field Exploration and Development. Thompson: Royal 8vo
                                       *Nearly Ready*
Oil Palm Cultivation. Milligan. Small Crown 8vo . . . . 3s
Ore Deposits of South Africa. Johnson.
    Part II.—The Witwatersrand and Pilgrimsrest Goldfields and
    Similar Occurrences. Demy 8vo . . . . . . . 5s
Packing-Case Tables. Richardson. Oblong 4to . . . . . 5s
Painting for the Imitation of Woods and Marbles. Van der Burg.
    Royal Folio . . . . . . . . . . . £3 3s
Paints : Their Chemistry and Technology. Toch. Royal 8vo . . 25s
Paper and its Uses. Dawe. Crown 8vo . . . . . 8s 6d
Paper-Making. Clapperton. Crown 8vo . . . . . 7s 6d
Paper-Making. Watt. Crown 8vo . . . . . . 8s 6d
Paper-Making, Chapters on. Beadle. 5 vols. Crown 8vo. Per vol. 6s
Pastrycook and Confectioner's Guide. Wells. Crown 8vo . . 2s
Pattern Making. Barrows. Crown 8vo . . . . . . 12s 6d
Pattern Making. Horner. Demy 8vo . . . *New Ed. Nearly Ready*
Perfumes and Cosmetics. Askinson. Medium 8vo . . . . 30s
Petrol Air Gas. O'Connor. Crown 8vo . . . . . 2s 6d
Petroleum and its Substitutes, Chemistry of. Tinkler and Chal-
    lenger. Medium 8vo . . . . . . . . . 15s
Petroleum, Oil Fields of Russia and the Russian Petroleum
    Industry. Beeby Thompson. Royal 8vo . . . . . 21s
Pigments. An Artists' Manual. Standage. Crown 8vo . . . 2s
Pigs and Bacon Curing. Davies. Crown 8vo . . . . 4s 6d
Plumbing. Blake. Crown 8vo. In two vols. . . . . *Each 6s*
Portland Cement, The Modern Manufacture of. West. Royal 8vo.
                                 *New Ed. Preparing*
Portuguese Dictionary. Elwes. Demy 12mo . . . . 8s 6d
Pot Plant Culture. Davidson. Crown 8vo. . . . . . 5s
Poultry Farming : Commercial. Toovey. Crown 8vo . . . 6s
Producer Gas Practice (American) and Industrial Gas Engineering.
    Latta. Demy 4to . . . . . . . . . . 30s
Propagation and Pruning. Newsham. Demy 8vo . . . . 6s
Prospecting. Merritt. Fcap. 8vo . . . . . . . 6s
Prospecting for Gold. Rankin. Fcap. 8vo . . . . . 7s 6d
Prospector's Handbook. Anderson. Small Crown 8vo . . . 5s

*All Published Prices are net.*

Pumps and Pumping. Bale. Crown 8vo . . . . . . 5s
Punches, Dies, and Tools. Woodworth. Medium 8vo . . . 25s
Quantities and Measurements. Beaton. Crown 8vo . . . . 2s 6d
Radio and High-Frequency Currents. Larner. Crown 8vo 3s 6d
Radiodynamics. Miessner. Crown 8vo . . . . . . . 12s
Radio-Communication, Elements of, Stone. Crown 8vo . . . 15s
Railway Points and Crossings. Dobson. Crown 8vo. . . . 6s
Rating and Assessment. Webb. Demy 8vo . . . . . 15s
Receipts, Formulas, and Processes. Hiscox. Medium 8vo . . 21s
Recoil of Guns. Rausenberger. Translated by Slater. Demy 8vo 12s 6d
Refrigerating and Ice-Making Pocket-Book. Wallis-Tayler. Cr. 8vo 5s
Refrigeration, Cold Storage, and Ice-Making. Wallis-Tayler. Med. 8vo 15s
Reinforced Concrete Bridges. Scott. Royal 8vo. . . *Nearly Ready*
Reinforced Concrete Design Simplified. Gammon & Dyson. Crown 4to 15s
Rivers without Embankments. Leete. Large Crown 4to . . . 30s
Road Engineering. Goldsmith. Demy 8vo . . . . *Nearly Ready*
Roads : The Making of Highroads. Carey. Crown 8vo . . 3s 6d
Roof Carpentry. Collings. Crown 8vo . . . . . . 2s 6d
Rothamsted Experiments. Tipper. Crown 8vo . . . . . 4s
Rubber : its Cultivation and Preparation. Johnson. *New Ed. Preparing*
Rubber Hand Stamps. Sloane. Square 8vo . . . . 7s 6d
Rubber Planter's Note-Book. Braham. Fcap. 8vo . . . . 5s
Safe Railway Working. Stretton. Crown 8vo . . . . 4s 6d
Safe Use of Steam. By an Engineer . . . . . . . 6d
Sailmaking. Sadler. 4to . . . . . . . . . 12s 6d
Sanitation, Water Supply, and Sewage Disposal of Country Houses.
        Gerhard. Crown 8vo . . . . . . . . . 12s 6d
Savouries and Sweets. Miss Allen. Fcap. 8vo . . . . 1s
Saw Mills. Bale. Demy 8vo . . . . . . . . . 15s
Screw Cutting for Engineers. Pull. Crown 8vo . . . 2s 6d
Screw Threads. Hasluck. Waistcoat-pocket size . . . . 2s
Sea Terms, Phrases, and Words. Pirrie. Fcap. 8vo . . . 7s 6d
Sewage, Purification of. Barwise. Demy 8vo . . . . 12s 6d
Sewerage Hydraulics. Coleman. Demy 8vo . . . . . 10s 6d
Sewerage of Sea Coast Towns. Adams. Demy 8vo . . . . 6s
Sewerage Systems. Watson and Herbert. Royal 8vo . . 12s 6d
Sheet Metal Worker's Instructor. Warn and Horner. Crown 8vo
                            *New Edition Nearly Ready*
Shipbuilding Industry of Germany. Felskowski. Super Royal 4to 10s 6d
Silver. The Metallurgy of. Eissler. Crown 8vo . . . . 12s 6d
Slide Rule. Hoare. Sm. Crown 8vo . . . . . . . 4s
Smoley's Tables—1. Logarithms and Squares. . . . . 27s
                  2. Slopes and Rises . . . . . . 24s
                  3. Logarithmic-Trigonometric Tables . . 6s
                  In one vol. complete. Thumb Index . . . 40s
Soap : Modern Soap and Detergent Industry. Martin. Royal 8vo
    Vol. 1   Theory and Practice of Soap Making . . . . 36s
    Vol. 2   Special Soaps and Detergent Compositions .*Nearly Ready*

*All Published Prices are net.*

Soap-Making. Watt. Crown 8vo . . . . . . . . 9s
Soap-Making Manual. Thomssen. 6" × 4½" . . . . 12s 6d
Soaps, Candles, and Glycerine. Lamborn. Medium 8vo . . . 54s
Solubilities of Inorganic and Organic Substances. Seidell. Med. 8vo 45s
Spanish Dictionary. Elwes. Demy 12mo . . . . . 6s
Spanish Grammar and Reader. Korth. Fcap. 8vo . . . 2s 6d
Specifications in Detail. Macey and Allen. Royal 8vo . . . 30s
Specifications for Practical Architecture. Bartholomew. Revised
   by Rogers. 8vo . . . . . . . . . . . 16s
Stanley, William Ford : His Life and Work. Inwards. Demy 8vo 2s 6d
Stationary Engines. Hurst. Crown 8vo . . . . . . 2s
Steam : The Application of Highly Superheated Steam to Loco-
   motives. Garbe. Edited by Robertson. Medium 8vo . . 9s
Steam Engine. Haeder and Powles. Crown 8vo . . . 10s 6d
Steam Engine. Goodeve. Crown 8vo . . . . . . 6s 6d
Steam Engine (Portable). Wansbrough. Demy 8vo . . . . 6s
Steam Engineering in Theory and Practice. Hiscox and Harrison.
   Medium 8vo . . . . . . . . . . . . 21s
Steel Research Committee's Report. Fcap. Folio . . . 31s 6d
Steel Square Applied to Roof Construction. Draper. Crown 8vo 2s 6d
Steel Thermal Treatment. Urquhart. Medium 8vo . . . . 35s
Steel : Elliott's Weights of Steel. Medium 8vo . . . . £2 10s
Stone Quarrying—Practical. Greenwell and Elsden. Med. 8vo . 15s
Stone Working Machinery. Bale. Crown 8vo . . . . 10s 6d
Strains, Handy Book for the Calculation of. Humber. Crown 8vo 7s 6d
Strains on Structures of Ironwork. Shields. 8vo . . . . 5s
Streamline Kite Balloons. Sumner. Medium 8vo . . . 10s 6d
Structural Engineer's Pocket Book. Andrews. Crown 8vo . . 18s
Submarine Torpedo Boat. Hoar. Crown 8vo . . . . . 12s
Superficial Measurement. Hawkings. Crown 8vo . . . . 4s
Survey Practice. Jackson. 8vo . . . . . . . 12s 6d
Surveying. Whitelaw. Demy 8vo . . . . . . . . 16s
Surveying for Settlers. Crosley. Small Crown 8vo . . 7s 6d
Surveying Sheets for Professional and Educational Use. Oblong
   Royal 8vo . . . . . . . . . . . 1s 6d
Surveying : Land and Engineering. Baker and Leston. . *Nearly Ready*
Surveying, Land and Marine. Haskoll. Large Crown 8vo . . 9s
Surveying, Land and Mining. Leston. Large Crown 8vo . 8s 6d
Surveying, Practical. Usill and Leston. Large Crown 8vo . 7s 6d
Surveying with the Tacheometer. Kennedy. Demy 8vo . . 12s 6d
Surveyor's Field Book for Engineers and Mining Surveyors.
   Haskoll. Crown 8vo . . . . . . . . . 12s 6d
Tanning Materials & Extract Manufacture. Harvey. Demy 8vo . 15s
Tanning (Practical). Rogers and Flemming. Medium 8vo . . 45s
Tannins (Synthetic). Grasser and Enna. Demy 8vo . . . 12s
Tea Machinery and Tea Factories. Wallis-Tayler. Medium 8vo . 28s
Technical Guide, Measurer, and Estimator. Beaton. Waistcoat-
   pocket size . . . . . . . . . . . . 2s

*All Published Prices are net.*

Technical Terms : English-French, French-English, Fletcher.
  Waistcoat-pocket size . . . . . . . . . . 2s
Technical Terms : English-German, German-English. Horner
  and Holtzmann. Waistcoat-pocket size . . . . 3s 6d
Technical Terms : English-Spanish, Spanish-English. Monteverde.
  Waistcoat-pocket size . . . . . . . . . 3s
Telephones : their Construction, Installation, Wiring, Operation,
  and Maintenance. Radcliffe and Cushing. Fcap. 8vo . . 9s
Telephones : Field Telephones and Telegraphs for Army Use.
  Stevens. Crown 8vo . . . . . . . . . 3s
Timber Merchant. Richardson. Fcap. 8vo . . . . . . 4s
Timber Merchant's Companion. Dowsing. Crown 8vo . . 3s 6d
Tools for Engineers and Woodworkers. Horner. Demy 8vo . 10s 6d
Traverse Tables. Lintern. Small Crown 8vo . . . . 3s 6d
Tropical Agriculture. Johnson. Demy 8vo . . . . . . 5s
Tunnelling. Prelini and Hill. Royal 8vo . . . . . . 18s
Tunnelling, Practical. Simms and Clark. Imp. 8vo . . . 21s
Tunnel Shafts. Buck. 8vo . . . . . . . . . 12s 6d
Ultraviolet Radiation. Luckiesh. Demy 8vo . . . . . 21s
Upholstering. Bitmead. Crown 8vo . . . . . . 2s 6d
Urban Traffic, Principles of. Stone. Crown 8vo . . . . 3s 6d
Valuation of Real Property. Webb. Demy 8vo . . *Nearly Ready*
Valuation of Real Property. Lamputt. Crown 8vo . . . 2s 6d
Valuation, Tabular Aids to. M'Caw and Lyons. Crown 8vo . . 5s
Vegetable Culture. Davidson. Crown 8vo . . . . . 4s 6d
Veterinary Aid. Archer. Crown 8vo . . . . . . 7s 6d
Wages Tables. Garbutt. Square Crown 8vo . . . . . 6s
Watchmaker's Handbook. Saunier. Crown 8vo . . . . 12s 6d
Watch Repairing. Garrard. Crown 8vo . . . . . . 6s
Water Engineering. Slagg. Crown 8vo . . . . . 7s 6d
Water, Flow of. Schmeer. Medium 8vo . . . . . . 18s
Water Power Engineering. Taylor. Royal 8vo . . *Nearly Ready*
Water Supplies. Rideal. Demy 8vo . . . . . . 8s 6d
Water Supplies (Emergency.) Thompson. Medium 8vo . . 21s
Water Supply of Cities and Towns. Humber. Imp. 4to . . £6 6s
Water Supply (Rural). Greenwell and Curry. Crown 8vo . . 6s
Weight Calculator. Harben. Royal 8vo . . . . . . 25s
Wells and Bore-holes. Dumbleton. Demy 8vo . . *Nearly Ready*
Wire Ropes for Hoisting. Crown 4to . . . . . . 20s
Wireless Telegraphy. Erskine-Murray. Demy 8vo  *New Ed. Preparing*
Wireless Telegraphy (Framework of). Cadilhac. Demy 8vo . 4s 6d
Wireless Telephones. Erskine-Murray. Crown 8vo . . 4s 6d
Wireless Telephony. Ruhmer. Demy 8vo . . . . 10s 6d
Wood, The Seasoning of. Wagner. Royal 8vo . . . . 21s
Wood-Carving for Amateurs. By a Lady. Crown 8vo . . 2s 6d
Woodworking Machinery. Bale. Large Crown 8vo . . 10s 6d
Woodworking Machinery for Small Workshops. Ball. Cr. 8vo 3s 6d
Workshop Practice, Modern. Pull. Large Crown 8vo . . 16s
Works' Manager's Handbook. Hutton. Medium 8vo . . 18s

*All Published Prices are net.*

# PRACTICAL HANDBOOKS FOR HOME STUDY.

### Issued by THE AMERICAN TECHNICAL SOCIETY.
### Agents: CROSBY LOCKWOOD & SON.

*NOTE.—The Prices herein quoted are based on American Prices and therefore subject to revision without notice.*

| | |
|---|---|
| Air Brake. Ludy | 7s 6d |
| Alternating-Current Machinery. Esty | 15s |
| Architectural Drawing and Lettering. Bourne | 7s 6d |
| Armature Winding. Moreton | 10s |
| Automobile Construction and Repair. Hall | 15s |
| Automobile Ignition, Starting and Lighting. Hayward | £2 |
| Bank Bookkeeping. Sweetland | 7s 6d |
| Blueprint Reading. Fairfield and Kenison | 10s |
| Bridge Engineering—Roof Trusses. Dufour | 15s |
| Building and Flying an Aeroplane. Hayward | 5s |
| Building Code. Fitzpatrick | 7s 6d |
| Building Superintendence. Nichols | 10s |
| Building Superintendence for Reinforced Concrete Structures. Post | 7s 6d |
| Building Superintendence for Steel Structures. Belden | 7s 6d |
| Business English and Correspondence. Barrett | 7s 6d |
| Carpentry. Townsend | 7s 6d |
| Civil Engineering Specifications and Contracts. Ashbridge | 10s |
| Commercial Law. Chamberlain | 10s |
| Compressed Air. Wightman | 7s 6d |
| Contracts and Specifications. Nichols | 7s 6d |
| Corporation Accounts and Voucher System. Griffith | 5s |
| Corporation Law. Abbott, Springer, and Gilmore | 15s |
| Cotton Spinning. Hedrick | 12s 6d |
| Dams and Weirs. Bligh | 10s |
| Descriptive Astronomy. Moulton | 10s |
| Electric Railways. Craveth | 7s 6d |
| Electric Lighting. Harrison | 10s |
| Electric and Gas Welding. Cravens | 7s 6d |
| Electrochemistry and Metallurgy. Burgess | 7s 6d |
| Electrochemistry and Welding. Burgess | 10s |
| Elements of Electricity. Millikan | 7s 6d |
| Elevators. Jallings | 12s 6d |
| Estimating. Nichols | 7s 6d |
| Fire Insurance Law. Hardy | 10s |
| Fireproof Construction. Fitzpatrick | 12s 6d |
| Ford Car. Bayston | 10s |
| Forging. Jernberg | 7s 6d |
| Foundry Work. Gray | 10s |
| Freehand and Perspective Drawing. Everett | 5s |
| Gas and Oil Engines and Gas Producers. Marks | 12s 6d |
| Gasoline Automobile. Lougheed | 7s 6d |
| Gasoline Tractors. Hayward | 7s 6d |
| Getting a Good Job. Barrett | 5s |

*All Published Prices are net.*

*All Published Prices are net.*

*Printed in Great Britain by* UNWIN BROTHERS, LIMITED, LONDON AND WOKING

# A SELECTED LIST OF WEALE'S SERIES.

*All Published Prices are net.*

# LONDON : CROSBY LOCKWOOD & SON,
## 7 STATIONERS' HALL COURT, LUDGATE HILL, E.C.4.